T0328095

MAX VERSTAPPEN

MAX VERSTAPPEN

THE UNSTOPPABLE FORCE IN FORMULA ONE

Ewan McKenzie

IVY PRESS

Quarto

First published in 2024 by Ivy Press,
an imprint of The Quarto Group.
One Triptych Place,
London, SE1 9SH,
United Kingdom
T (0)20 7700 6700
www.Quarto.com

A catalogue record for this book is
available from the British Library.

ISBN 978-0-7112-9492-9
Ebook ISBN 978-0-7112-9493-6

10 9 8 7 6 5 4 3 2 1

Design by Cara Rogers
Cover design by Daisy Woods
Printed in China

MIX
Paper | Supporting
responsible forestry
FSC
www.fsc.org   FSC® C016973

CONTENTS

INTRODUCTION

In the 2023 Formula 1 season Max Verstappen was unstoppable. He had been irresistible the season before, but as the results piled up in his ninth year of F1 racing, records began to tumble. Equipped with the Red Bull RB19 he broke seemingly unattainable records for most successive wins and most wins in a season. And this was supposed to be the year when the rest of the grid caught up...

Like tennis player Rafa Nadal, Max's childhood was dominated by a close family member who could push their young charge to the limit, sometimes beyond. Jos Verstappen was by far the biggest Dutch F1 star and his big break came before he was ready – a rookie paired with all-time-great, Michael Schumacher. Jos was determined that Max would learn from the mistakes he had made in his racing career.

Right from his early karting days, Jos administered tough love to his son. Max's supreme talent behind the wheel was plain to see... provided he could keep his impatience in check. Jos kept Max out of the driver programmes, preferring to retain control over his destiny, and after just one season of single-seater racing in European Formula 3, stepped up to the big time.

When Max was promoted to Toro Rosso at 17 many in the F1 paddock thought it was ridiculous. Verstappen 2.0 has proved them all wrong. This is the story of Max's journey from howling four-year-old at the side of a kart track to a three-time world champion, who many view as unbeatable. In between are ten stand-out races that have helped seal his enviable reputation.

Max is not in the mould of the moody, introspective F1 star. Fame and wealth have hardly changed him. Helmut Marko compares him to Ayrton Senna, but you would hardly find the great Brazilian dressing up in lederhosen for the Austrian Grand Prix, or getting his face painted for the Mexican 'Day of the Dead'.

In 2024 Max is unlikely to stop teasing his race engineer when he wants to attempt the fastest lap at the end of the race. 'Sometimes no risk is no fun, you have to spice it up a bit. That's a motto Dietrich (Red Bull founder) used to use. No risk, no fun. So I'm going to implement that.'

He has said in the past that he's not in Formula 1 for the records, to see where he fits 'between other people's names or the greats in the sport'. Very soon, he will have to replace 'between' for 'on top of'...

RIGHT: Max races ahead of Adrian Newey as the Red Bull team celebrate Max Verstappen's ninth win in a row at the 2023 Dutch Grand Prix.

DOUBLE DUTCH

There are many sons of racing drivers who start in karting, the bottom rung of the motorsport ladder. There are many who make it to the junior formulae – Formula Renault, Formula 4 and Formula 3. Not so many make it into the high-pressured world of grand prix support races, Formula 2, where race budgets can approach $3million. There are fewer still who make it onto the Formula 1 grid, and, as Mick Schumacher can verify, having a famous racing father may open doors, but those doors don't stay open very long.

Only four sons of racing drivers have gone on to become world champions – Damon Hill, Jacques Villeneuve and Nico Rosberg, each with a single championship to their name. Max Verstappen is the fourth, with three titles... and counting. But then again Max has an advantage over all of them. He is not the son of one racing driver, he is the son of two.

Jos Verstappen grew up in Limburg, the southernmost of the Netherlands' twelve provinces, which juts like a narrow peninsula between Belgium to the west and Germany to the east. His father Frans owned a bar in Montfort, Café de Rotonde on the roundabout in the centre of town, and his grandfather Sjef ran a scrapyard. Frans ran a karting team in his spare time. There was little or no history of single-seater motor-racing from that part of the country, with the focus of attention at Zandvoort up on the North Sea coast.

Jos had a difficult relationship with his father, both being cut from the same uncompromising cloth, and the two often came to blows. It resulted in Jos bunking off to his grandfather's yard to mess about with car engines and avoid his father. When Jos showed an interest in karting, it was up to him to work on the karts and tune them up.

Despite the lack of family finance, Jos's ability to drive a kart at speed was apparent. His talent behind the wheel helped him become Dutch karting champion in 1984 and 1986. The nearest karting track to Montfort was across the border in Genk, 45km away, and to spend more time with his karts, Paul Lemmens, owner of the track, gave Jos a job preparing the rental karts, allowing him to spend more time practising out on a circuit that both his employee and his employee's son would later star on.

Sophie Kumpen, Max's mum, was also a karting prodigy, but across the border in Belgium. Genk was her local track. Coming from a wealthier background than the Verstappens, her family were far more invested in motor-sport – her cousin Anthony Kumpen also took up karting and has gone on to compete in the NASCAR Xfinity series, the GT Championship and raced at Le Mans.

Ironically, Red Bull boss Christian Horner, a former driver himself, was well aware of Sophie's driving talents long before Max came into the world. 'I raced against Max's mum in 1989 in the Junior Kart World Championship,' he told the *Finanacial Times*. 'In that race, there were some super-talented drivers: Jan Magnussen, Jarno Trulli, Giancarlo Fisichella and Dario Franchitti. She was top 10 in the world, for sure.' In fact she finished ninth in that championship.

World champion Jenson Button was also a fan: 'Sophie, Max's mum, was a fantastic driver when I was racing in karts in 1995. She was my team-mate so I saw her drive,' he told a Beyond The Grid podcast. 'I knew how good she was. It was her and the late Lotta Hellberg – those two were just awesome.'

Sophie grew up in Hasselt, only a few kilometres from the Genk track, and so it's easy to see how her world collided with the charismatic Dutchman everyone was tipping for great things in Formula 1.

RIGHT: Jos Verstappen studies the timing screen in the Benetton garage.

BELOW: The calamitous 1994 pitlane fire that could have had fatal consequences.

They were married in 1996 when Sophie was 20 and Jos was 24, already an established name on the F1 grid. Max was born a year later when his mum was just 21, and at that age babies can arrive fast. In September 1997 Jos Verstappen had a loyal Dutch fanbase running a website for him and he dutifully reported to his fans that Max Emillian Verstappen had arrived in 40 minutes on the 30 September. Even as a baby Max was quick.

The website editor predicted with unusual prescience: 'If Max has inherited the racing talents of both of his parents then a new Formula 1 driver for the year 2020 has been born.' Max would emerge in a Formula 1 car by the year 2014 – six years premature.

Though she did go on to race in Suzuki Swifts, the arrival of Max and sister Victoria in 1999 effectively put an end to Sophie Kumpen's racing ambitions while Jos tried to make an impression on the F1 world stage. It was this agonizing journey of Jos in the world of single-seater racing that would give him the experience to guide Max in the future. It would also create the Vercrashen/Jos the Boss reputation that would spark interest in his son. Jos moved from his karting triumphs into racing cars with exactly the same buzz that his son would generate two decades later.

Having won his debut single-seater series, the Benelux Formula Vauxhall-Lotus of 1992 at the age of 20, he set his sights on the German Formula 3 series for 1993. Jos won eight times, finished on the podium 14 times in the 20 races and clinched the championship in his first year. What delighted his Dutch fans even more was that he won the Marlboro Dutch Masters race, a one-off event held at Zandvoort, with free entry for fans (courtesy of the big bucks paid by a tobacco sponsor).

So there was particular Dutch interest when the hotshot from Limburg was invited to test an F1 car, the Footwork-Mugen Honda. From a racing perspective it was a huge leap in power from the 175bhp generated by a Formula 3 car to the 750bhp of a Formula 1 car with the sophistication of traction control, active suspension, semi-automatic gearbox and, most impressive of all to an F1 debutant, incredibly efficient carbon brakes that had them pressed tight into their six-point harness (as used in a jet fighter).

Covering the event for *Autosport* Andy Hallbery wrote, 'Verstappen has built a reputation for climbing into a car and stunning onlookers with his immediate pace'. A description that would be echoed and amplified for his son twenty years later. 'The instructions from the team were clear and simple. Take your time, make sure you are comfortable and find your limit.'

Staying within limits is hardly the Verstappen way. By the end of the afternoon Jos had completed 65 laps of the Estoril track with a best of 1m14.45s, good enough for 10th on the grid for the recent Portuguese Grand Prix and just 0.07s slower than regular driver Derek Warwick. Derek Warwick, lest it be forgotten, was the man who Ayrton Senna blocked as his Lotus team-mate, because he was too quick.

With the news of the Footwork test immediately relayed to the paddock, F1 teams were soon on the phone to Jos's manager, the ex-F1 driver Huub Rothengatter. When you're hot in F1, you're very hot. The typical progress of any aspiring F1 driver would be Formula 3, a season or two in Formula 3000 (the equivalent of today's F2) and then the jump to Formula 1. Jos was immediately offered a one-year deal testing for the Benetton F1 team run by Flavio Briatore.

The financial landscape of Formula 1 was quite different in the 1990s, with unrestricted budgets and shadow test teams, separate from the race teams, trying

LEFT: Jos with manager Huub Rothengatter during his time at the Footwork team in 1996. Huub would be instrumental in Max's meteoric rise.

new developments out on the car throughout the season. Whereas today testing is limited to two periods on track before the first race and new parts run on the simulator, Verstappen was being signed up for a year of running round European circuits, giving feedback on tweaks to the Benetton B194. When time permitted, regular drivers Schumacher and Lehto would come along to give their input, but most of the hard yards would be done by Jos.

But then regular driver JJ Lehto fractured a vertebra in a Silverstone test crash and Jos was catapulted into his first F1 drive alongside Michael Schumacher. Jos had just turned 22 when he made his debut at the Brazilian Grand Prix in March 1994 at Interlagos. Not only was he being asked to line up alongside the fast and fearless Schumacher, he was doing so with minimal experience of the car, and what nobody knew at the time – though Ayrton Senna suspected – the likelihood that Michael had illegal traction control installed on his car.

It didn't help that on his debut Jos attempted an overtaking move on Eddie Irvine's Jordan, only for the inexperienced Ulsterman to fail to see him coming, swerve into his path and force Jos onto the grass. The Dutchman's car skeetered back onto the track causing a four-car accident that was not of his making.

Later in the year, at the German Grand Prix, Jos was involved in the biggest F1 refuelling fire of all time. It was yet another controversy that would engulf the Benetton team that year. To speed up pit-stops they had illegally removed a fuel filter from the standard refuelling rig and when the system failed at Hockenheim,

RIGHT: Jos sharing the podium with Damon Hill and Michael Schumacher at the 1994 Hungarian Grand Prix. It was the first ever Dutch podium, a record Max couldn't emulate in his rookie season.

racing fuel spilled out over the car and the pitlane. When it reached the engine of Jos's B194 it ignited in a split second into an enormous fireball that scorched the retreating pitcrew and threatened to put an end to the Verstappen racing dynasty before it had even begun.

'I remember coming in for what I thought was a routine pit-stop,' Verstappen recounted. 'Sitting in the car, I would open my visor at stops because when I was stationary I would sweat a lot. So as I came to a stop, I opened my helmet to get some fresh air. Then I saw the fluid coming. Then everything went up in flames and it was suddenly dark and black, and I couldn't breathe, like you are suddenly put in a dark room, and then you think, "I need to get out..."

'It was a struggle to get the steering wheel off, and that took me a couple of seconds. Then I had to release the belts. So there were a lot of things I had to do before I stood up and realized what had happened.' The fire was put out in seconds, but the incident made the television news across the globe.

In truth Jos didn't like the car, which had been designed to suit Schumacher's driving style, describing it as 'very nervous and difficult to drive', and though he scored two podium finishes, in Hungary and Belgium (also two of Max's more successful tracks), he was replaced by Johnny Herbert for 1995 and loaned out by Benetton to the Simtek team.

He switched to TWR-Arrows for 1996, finishing the season with 12 retirements from 16 races and a best finish of sixth in Argentina before joining Tyrrell in 1997, where he haunted the last two rows of the qualifying grid for most of the season.

He was left without a drive for 1998 when the team signed the under-talented-but-monied Ricardo Rosset (who Verstappen had comprehensively beaten as a team-mate at Arrows). He found a mid-season drive at Stewart when Jan Magnussen was fired, then sat out 1999 when the promising Honda F1 project he was signed up to was shelved.

Technical director of the Honda project, Harvey Postlethwaite was a

BELOW: Jos with wife Sophie Kumpen in the back seat of the two-seater Minardi in 2003. The car was designed to give passengers an experience of F1 acceleration and braking.

fan of Verstappen and had worked with him at Tyrrell. He had designed cars for Hesketh, Williams and Ferrari in his career and was also the man who had spotted the potential in Adrian Newey and given the Red Bull designer his first job in F1. But when Postlethwaite died from a heart attack, Honda's move into F1 was mothballed and Jos was out of a job.

Verstappen returned to the Tom Walkinshaw fold for a second stint at Arrows in 2000 and was retained for a second season for the first time in his career in 2001, scoring its only point with a sixth place in Austria (another strong Max track). Manager Huub Rothengatter failed to secure him a drive for 2002, but he returned to the grid in 2003 with Paul Stoddart's European Minardi team, racing at the back of the grid with an under-resourced team. A ninth-place finish in Canada was the best result of his final year in F1, though he did get to drive guests in the European-Minardi two-seater, most importantly his wife, Sophie.

In an ironic twist of fate, a few years later, in 2005, Stoddart sold his Minardi team to the Red Bull organization who decided to run it under the name Toro Rosso. Hence Jos Verstappen's final F1 team would ultimately become his son's first. And if you like to see the bounds of F1 genealogy stretched further, he also drove for Stewart Grand Prix, which was taken over and renamed Jaguar, which was bought by Dietrich Mateschitz and became Red Bull.

BELOW: Jos racing for the Netherlands' team during the shortlived A1 GP series which ran from 2005 to 2006.

So, Jos Verstappen retired from the pinnacle of motorsport with two podiums to his name, having raced across eight seasons for six teams and started 106 races. He may not have re-written any record books, other than surviving the most calamitous pitlane fire, but he had already surpassed all contenders for the greatest Dutch F1 driver of all time. In Holland, he was still a star name, writing a motorsport column for leading newspaper *De Telegraaf*. In F1 he was a byword for unfulfilled talent, someone who got his big break too early. There would be other drives – in the nation vs nation A1 GP series where he represented the Netherlands – but essentially that was it. Two outings at Le Mans in 2008 and 2009 were the final topline drives.

One of Verstappen Senior's greatest abilities was running and tuning kart engines. His informal apprenticeship at Paul Lemmens' Genk race track had served him well. A successful career behind the wheel of a kart also helped optimize a kart's performance, because drivers get to vary the carburettor of the machines, something that Max would get to learn. Jos had started his kart-racing team in parallel to his F1 career and the kudos of the Verstappen name certainly helped attract eager karting hopefuls.

Max grew up in and around karting paddocks, often riding around on a pedal kart or a quad bike his parents bought him when he was two years old. Jos was reluctant to buy his son a kart until he was around six years old, reasoning that he would quickly grow out of any small kart and he'd have to buy a new one soon after.

In 2002 he was 'in between' F1 drives, but still visiting teams and showing his face round the paddock. Max didn't give up on pestering his parents. Jos continued to say no. Then the defining moment came when, at the age of four-and-a-half, Max discovered that his friend, Stan Pex – a year younger than Max – had been given a go-kart. The Pex family and the Verstappens have been close karting friends for years and Max is still close to both Stan and Jorrit Pex.

Jos was away at a Formula 1 race in Canada when he got the call from Sophie. 'My wife called me and said that he was standing by her side crying, because he wanted to drive. But I wanted to wait until he was about six. But no, he was insistent. So I bought him a kart. We still have it. It's hanging in the shop (the Verstappen Store in Swalmen) where we sell the merchandise.'

The family were living in Sophie's home town of Hasselt, where Max was born, so naturally, the first track Max drove on was nearby Genk. The smallest and least risky circuit at Genk was the rental track and true to form Max wasted no time in

ABOVE: Once Jos's driving career was over he dedicated most of his time to Max's karting progress.

putting his foot down. Even Jos was surprised at the pace of his son. He knew he had good control of speed through braking and accelerating of the quad bike, but this was a revelation.

'I remember after a few laps, he did the whole track flat out. And because of the vibration of the kart the carburettor was falling off all the time. We did it for one day, and then immediately bought him a bigger go-kart.'

The structure of kart racing is strictly governed by age. Although Max could zip round tracks and demonstrate his speed and scare his mother in his newly acquired toy he couldn't officially race until 30 September 2004.

The journey to F1 began when Max was seven years old at a small kart track in Emmen in the north of Holland close to the German border. Jos discovered that he was not only a competitive dad, he was a nervous competitive dad. Unlike Michael Schumacher's son Mick, who first raced under the name Mick Betsch (Corinna Betsch is Mick's mum), Max was racing as a Verstappen... in the

Netherlands... and everyone would want to beat the son of the most famous Dutch racing driver.

'My dad was more nervous than me, which was funny,' Max relates, 'I could see him next to the fence each time I came round, and you could see from his body language that he was really tense and worried.'

Max got pole and won both races in his category, a result repeated again and again. In fact his constant success, winning the first 68 of 70 kart races, started to generate rumours that the Verstappens had some unfair advantage, maybe an illegal kart. What Team Verstappen did have was a highly skilled kart engineer/ supreme kart-driving coach, combined with a fearless pilot who'd been handling speed since he was in kindergarten. No wonder the package was unbeatable.

From running his own kart team, Jos soon realized that Max could well become the Netherlands' second most successful F1 driver and concentrated his efforts on his son. 'I was always racing with him, my social life was basically not there. I was his mechanic, van driver, engine tuner, seven days a week,' he told *Top Gear* magazine. 'It was more like a job, 8am until 10pm, I was hardly at home. I think I made more sacrifices, preparing everything.'

Karting is structured around the power of machines and, as children get older, so they become eligible for karts with more powerful, higher revving engines and grippier tyres which increase cornering speed. Max's success followed a repeated pattern, as each time he became eligible for the next category he would enter and win, often competing against children two or three years older than himself.

BOTTOM LEFT: Young Max met ex-karter Jenson Button when he visited the Genk kart track.

BELOW: Max came up against Jenson in F1 from the 2015 season. This photo is from Monaco 2017.

BOTTOM RIGHT: Don't be fooled by the baby face, Max proved to be a fearless karter from the moment he got behind the wheel.

By the age of 12 he was starting to compete in European championships, driving KF karts which are continuous drive karts (i.e. no gear changing) with KF3 the slowest and KF1 the fastest. Beyond that was the top category, the F1 of karting, KZ karts, which had a six-speed gearbox and a water-cooled 125cc engine. You needed to be 15 years old to race in a KZ kart, but drivers could compete in both KF and KZ championships when they got to that age.

From his debut until 2009 it would be Jos and Max at the track, week in week out, with Jos taking advantage of space in friend Richard Pex's Maasbracht workshop to prepare and fine-tune his son's karts. But after winning everything in range of Limburg it was time to widen Max's sporting horizon.

Two significant problems arose along the way that could have derailed the karting prodigy. After the marital arguments became too much, his parents were divorced in 2008. They agreed that sister Victoria would live with Sophie in Hasselt. Max would live with Jos in Maaseik, still in Belgium but close to Maasbracht and a clog's throw from Genk. But it was not easy for Sophie. 'I let Max go because I knew that if he wanted to make a career he would have to go with Jos. That was very emotional for me because you're letting go of your child... At a certain point I didn't really know Max as a teenager.'

That didn't mean to say his mum would be absent from Max's future races. At key events, she would take Victoria (also a keen karter) to support her son. But as Max moved up to race in European series the chance to watch her son regularly became more limited. It didn't help that the short-tempered Jos was given a

restraining order for sending abusive text messages to his ex-wife and would appear in court to be found guilty of breaking that order.

The second problem Max encountered was school. Finding time to practise, race and complete secondary school work at Saint Ursula's was tricky and required an obliging school attitude. Jos estimates that they would travel between 80 and 100,000 kilometres a year to races in France, Germany, the UK and the hotbed of the karting world, Italy – which wasn't a problem in the school holidays, but term time was different. Max was obliged to study subjects he had no intention of following up.

It was the same for all his karting peers, and the subject of a surprise 'mini-rant' by Red Bull's Adrian Newey at a technical briefing before the 2014 Belgian Grand Prix. Five days after the Red Bull organization had announced the signing of Max for the 2015 season Newey was asked to comment on the fast-reducing ages of F1 drivers. 'I think what is a much more concerning question is the effect on their education... A lot of the drivers in karting and in junior formulas frankly just aren't going to school. The parents then hide behind that by saying that they have private tutors but I think in many cases that's actually a complete sham.

'Being at a motor race and so forth, the kids do learn in a different way – not an academic way but they learn in other ways – but I think for many of those children that don't quite make the grade, they have spent all that time not going to school, not having a proper tuition and then what happens to them afterwards is altogether another question.'

That question would not arise for Max, a teenage multi-millionaire. Though a lack of classroom time might well explain his reluctance to dive deep into technical debriefs – even in karting there was data that could be studied in depth and neither Max nor Jos were keen to go down that route of studying telemetry, they wanted to experience the circuit at first hand.

The karters that Max came up against during his time in European competition represent a golden period for the sport, with many graduating to F1 careers. Not exactly 'the Brat Pack', more like 'the Kart Pack'. Charles Leclerc, Alex Albon, Pierre Gasly, Nyck de Vries, George Russell, Lando Norris and Esteban Ocon all know each other from kart meetings in Europe where they raced against each other, or were in age groups above or below. Max also raced Anthoine Hubert, the Formula 2 racer tipped for an F1 seat who was killed in a Formula 2 race at Spa in 2019.

Max had a famous encounter with Charles Leclerc in a KF2 race at Val d'Argenton, a circuit north-west of Poitiers in western France. The pair had a coming together during a wet qualifying session where Max was challenging series leader Leclerc and they had a bit of wheel-to-wheel action. Max got a friendly bump from behind while in front of Charles on track and they indulged in a touch of wheel banging after that. It finally resulted in Max spinning off and race officials disqualifying them both. Max wasn't amused but Charles has fond memories of the 'racing incident'. 'He ended up on the grass,' Leclerc recalls, 'his kart went in such a deep puddle that only his helmet was sticking out of the water! He was really furious. Now, thinking back to that episode makes me laugh a lot.'

TOP LEFT: Max with his great karting rival Charles Leclerc, during the time he was an Intrepid factory driver.

TOP RIGHT: Max spent most of his karting career as a CRG driver. Here he is with a cheeky, smiling chappy at far left. That's Lando Norris.

FAR LEFT: Max came up against Alex Albon in the junior formulae.

LEFT: Another karting buddy was fellow Dutch star Nyck de Vries. Nyck is actually two years older than Max.

Max would ultimately get the last laugh by becoming the first of the kart-pack to get into F1, and before that he would need to prove himself by winning some European karting championships. Along the way dad Jos would show him what David Coulthard has characterized as some 'tough love'.

An ideal opportunity presented itself at the 2012 Karting World Cup in Sarno, near Naples in Italy, a 3,400-kilometre round trip from the Verstappens' Dutch base. Jos knew Max had the ability to clinch it. After some typical battling performances in the KZ2 heats, Max put his kart on pole for the final. But on the second lap he got passed by Daniel Bray. His mindset back then was to immediately try and get the lead back and he made a far-too-optimistic move on

the leading kart that saw him crash into the back of his rival and out of the race. Karting is all about slipstreaming, passing and repassing, yet Max had rushed it and his race – and the chance of a landmark win – was over.

'It was a bit stupid and unnecessary,' Max admits. 'My dad had invested so much time already the years before, preparing the engines, making sure that once I stepped up to a category, that everything would be ready to go. So I was of course upset, but my dad was really upset and disappointed in me.'

Jos struggles to hide emotions such as 'upset and disappointed'. He was ragingly angry.

'He broke down the tent, everything, he threw it in the van,' recalled Max in a Red Bull podcast. 'I had to pick up the kart with a friend of mine on the track after the race because my dad said I had to do it myself. We sat in the van on our way back home. I wanted to talk to my dad about what happened, my opinion about the incident, but he didn't want to talk to me.

'I kept trying and at one point we stopped at a service station and he's saying to me: "Get out, I don't want to talk to you any more".'

And then Jos drove off, leaving the teenager behind in the middle of Europe. As it happened, Sophie Kumpen was behind them on the autoroute and would have been able to pick up her son, but when the red mist had retreated, Jos returned to pick him up. They didn't talk about it for the rest of the journey and Jos wouldn't speak to him the following week.

'I wanted him to understand that he had to think,' Jos reasons. 'The season afterwards we won everything. We won two European Championships, the World Championship, we won every race. He was so focused, the way he was racing you could see he was thinking, and I think because of what happened at that race, it made him a better driver.'

Other instances include Jos making Max drive in the cold with freezing hands and one time bashing him over the helmet in the paddock in full view of the other competitors. For a man whom his father Frans once described as 'loose with his hands' that was a dangerous approach, but Max is often the first to spring to his father's defence about his training approach.

Looking back at his junior career with Dutch website Autovise.nl in 2015, Max revealed. 'We always did everything together and he's been a huge support to me. Without him I wouldn't be here now.'

And the lessons Jos taught him left their mark. 'I dealt with setbacks in the lower divisions. I experienced it in my karting days, so I can easily move past that now.

LEFT: Jos stands over Max's kart at the fateful kart meeting in Sarno, Italy. Max is about to make an ill-timed overtaking move that would end his race early.

LEFT: In the paddock for the 2011 Belgian Grand Prix, the focus is on Jos Verstappen and partner Kelly van der Waal, who would become Max's stepmum and mother of his half-sister, Blue Jaye.

RIGHT: Max's supreme skill in the wet was honed during his karting career.

I'm never satisfied with my performance. And that's necessary. If I were complacent, I wouldn't improve.'

Jos Verstappen responded to criticism of his actions in the documentary, *Whatever It Takes.* 'People say how bad a father I was to him, to abuse your child,' he said. 'I never abused him.'

Jos believes the treatment was necessary for his son to learn how to become a competitive driver. 'I was teaching him. I was hard on him to make him learn. To make him think. A lot of people have no idea what you have to do to arrive at the top of a sport.'

The extent to which sports coaches can or should push young people is a growing debate in the coaching world, but Max's 'tough love' path to success has parallels with tennis player Rafa Nadal. Growing up in Mallorca, Nadal was coached by his uncle Toni. In the 2011 biography, *Rafa: My Story,* he recalls what it was like to be guided by a close relation.

'Toni was tough on me right from the start, tougher than the other children. He demanded a lot of me, pressured me hard. He'd use rough language, he'd shout a lot, he'd frighten me – especially when the other boys didn't turn up and it was just

the two of us. If I saw I'd be alone with him when I arrived for training, I'd get a sinking feeling in my stomach.'

Toni would order Rafa to sweep the clay courts after each session and if his concentration drifted, Toni would bombard him with tennis balls. Nadal now believes that this harsh regime helped to build up his resilience and mental strength he later displayed in professional matches.

Max and his exacting father never came to blows, but the younger Verstappen was often regarded as 'too relaxed for his own good'. There was a certain amount of pushback from the teenager. 'Pushing myself to the limits, the travelling, going all over the place,' Max recalls, 'it was just so intense. It was a bit like, why does it need to be like this?'

They would go for a practice session in Germany, pack the kart up afterwards and as they started home for Maaseik, the rain would start to fall. Instead of thinking that they got lucky with the weather, Jos would turn the van round, so that they could head back to the track for some running in the wet. 'For my dad, it didn't matter if it was warm, cold, dry, wet, he was out there saying things like "every lap you're making a mistake in that corner, you're just not doing it right". He was always constantly trying to improve me. Sometimes you take it a bit easier than others. And sometimes it got a bit heated.'

Max's Favourite Race

The 2013 season was Max Verstappen's defining season of kart-racing. He was now 15 and able to compete in the most powerful karts. His eight-year apprenticeship began to pay off. He won both the European KZ1 and KF1 championships, often racing against his close friend Jorrit Pex. The wins and the Verstappen name began to spark interest in the higher formulae of motor-racing – where would he be going next?

Jos's old racing manager Huub Rothengatter was similarly intrigued by the younger Verstappen's progress and wanted to see him in action. He and Raymond Vermeulen drove to Varennes-sur-Allier, north of Clermont-Ferrand in France, to watch Max in the KZ1 world championship final. A normally reclusive man who shuns interviews, Rothengatter was fulsome in his praise of Max. 'I heard all kinds of stories and saw great results this season. That made me want to see with my own eyes what Max was doing,' he said. And what Max was doing, was winning in style. Rothengatter's involvement and belief was important because he would be a vital element in Max's progress through the single-seater ranks.

Max was driving a factory CRG machine and team manager Euan Jeffery described the race in the official CRG press release: 'Max led a stunning race. He didn't start too well but then little by little he patiently built his victory. He showed his growth this year also in terms of race strategy. Building such a solid lead on a circuit like this shows his superiority.'

Despite having clocked up many great races in F3 and F1 Max still rates this one as his best victory, even though he described it at the time as 'easy': 'It's amazing, I didn't think it would have been so easy in the final as this track is all about slipstreaming. I have to thank CRG for the chassis, I was very happy with its balance as well as with my dad's engine that was perfect. I won all the championships, so it's been a perfect season. In November I will try to get the last international title of the season, KF world championship in Bahrain. I'm currently leading the standings and I hope I will manage to get such an important result to me and to the whole team.'

That title was the one that eluded him, beaten in the final by Brit Tom Joyner. But already Max's next step in motorsport had been taken...

TOP RIGHT: Max competing in the 2013 Winter Series at South Garda. Early in his career Jos had got Max practising with cold hands.

RIGHT: Max winning in the 2013 KF world championship; this round held at PF International, Lincolnshire.

A NEW
FORMULA

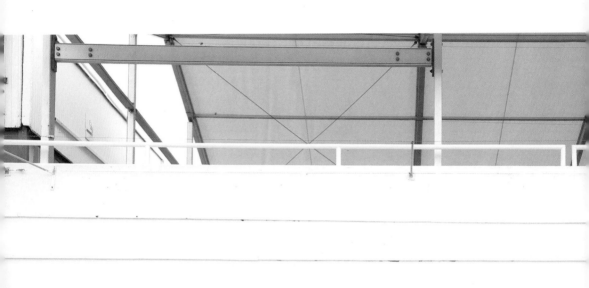

PREVIOUS PAGE:
Max leads the European Formula 3 race at the Moscow Raceway in July 2014.

LEFT: The Van Amersfoort Racing garages at the official European F3 test at the Hungaroring.

Before Max Verstappen finished his karting career he had already tested a Formula Renault car. His first outing in a single-seater racing car was a hush-hush event set up by Jos with Eric Boullier of Renault/Lotus, who apart from his involvement in F1 was a driver talent scout. Boullier had seen Max's potential from his karting performances and through his Renault connections he had arranged for the Dutch Manor MP Motorsport team to provide a Formula Renault 2.0 for Max. The test would be held at the 2.4km Pembrey circuit in South Wales.

Zandvoort would have been a far more convenient location, but Jos was keen to keep this moment low-key, especially with the Dutch media. He invited along Frits van Eldik, a veteran Dutch photographer he'd known from his racing days. The photos would be useful to promote Max to sponsors for his next step in motorsport. That would require finance above and beyond his karting budget. He would keep the news for his monthly motorsport column in *De Telegraaf*. He was yet to learn about his son's astonishing ability to absorb pressure.

It wouldn't be the first time that the old airfield race track had been used for a clandestine test. In the late 1980s, when testing in Formula 1 was not restricted, the McLaren team were regular visitors to the circuit. It was far enough off the beaten track not to attract the attention of the media, especially when you had the likes of Ayrton Senna in the car. Late in 1988 Senna was just over a month away from winning the first of his three F1 world championships when he came to Pembrey to test engines for the following season.

However, word got out and all of a sudden camera crews arrived on the track to record the great Brazilian, who would return to Pembrey many times. His lap of 44.43 seconds still stands as the lap record to this day.

'It's a high-grip surface which is nice to drive. It's quite twisty, so it's demanding,' Senna revealed. 'You have to put in a lot of effort, with physical and mental concentration all the time. It's a short lap, but for testing, it's a good circuit.'

Max's first day was wet, but that didn't stop the team bolting on some wet weather tyres and sending him out to learn the circuit. As has been the case for most of his motorsport life, when asked to go out and take things easy in a new car, Max tried to find the limits as quickly as he could. The mark MP Motorsport were expecting him to reach for a decent time in the changeable conditions was a 58-second lap on the short testing track.

By the end of a rain-soaked day he had managed to put in an impressive 56.1-second lap. The following day the rain cleared and Max set the fastest time for a 2013-spec Formula Renault 2.0 that anyone had recorded at Pembrey – and the car was still in one piece.

Further tests followed as Formula Renault teams weighed up their driver choice for 2014 while the Verstappens assessed which team would be the best home for their racing prodigy. On 9 and 10 October Max went to Hockenheim in Germany to test with the Belgian KTR team run by Kurt Mollekens. On 15 and 16 October Max was invited by the Finnish Koiranen GP team to test their Formula Renault car on the circuit at Alcarras near Barcelona.

BELOW: Jos and Max make a face-showing visit to the F1 paddock for the 2013 German GP at the Nürburgring.

In the rookie test at the Circuit de Catalunya he joined 32 other young hopefuls (not all of them rookies) and in the morning set third fastest time behind George Russell, before planting his car in the gravel and limiting progress. He ended up the day eighth. A week later he was in Hungary testing for the French team, Tech 1, against another future F1 star, Alex Albon. The British-Thai driver had already completed two seasons in Formula Renault yet Max beat his fastest time. At Spa-Francorchamps he was one of 19 drivers in an FR 2.0 car and beat them all in the wet and in the dry. By December 2013 he had tested nine times in Formula Renault, three of which were for Tech 1, who had won the title

F1'S YOUNGEST POLESITTERS

Max has recorded a podium and a win in eight consecutive seasons from 2016 to 2023

SEBASTIAN VETTEL
21 years, 72 days
2008 Italian Grand Prix

CHARLES LECLERC
21 years, 165 days
2019 Bahrain Grand Prix

FERNANDO ALONSO
21 YEARS, 236 DAYS
2003 Malaysian Grand Prix

MAX VERSTAPPEN
21 years, 307 days
2019 Hungarian Grand Prix

LANDO NORRIS
21 years, 316 days
2021 Russian Grand Prix

LANCE STROLL
22 years, 16 days
2020 Turkish Grand Prix

RUBENS BARRICHELLO
22 years, 97 days
1994 Belgian Grand Prix

LEWIS HAMILTON
22 years, 153 days
2007 Canadian Grand Prix

ANDREA DE CESARIS
22 years, 308 days
1982 United States Grand Prix West

NICO HULKENBERG
23 years, 79 days
2010 Brazilian Grand Prix

that year with another of his old karting rivals, Pierre Gasly. Still Team Verstappen were undecided.

Then came another offer to test, one which they couldn't turn down. In mid-December the Motopark team were testing F3 cars at the Ricardo Tormo circuit in Valencia, Spain. Would Max like to see if he could handle a little more power in the series above Formula Renault? He would.

'Max Verstappen has finished his first Formula 3 test day on a high,' reported Danny Sosel for Dutch motorsport website GPToday. 'The 16-year-old Dutchman made his F3 debut after nine tests with a Formula Renault 2.0 car. During the day, the four sessions were dominated by the son of Jos Verstappen. Tom Blomqvist was the only driver who could stay close to the Dutchman. The test day ended perfectly with Verstappen setting the fastest time ever for a Formula 3 car on the Ricardo Tormo Circuit in Valencia.'

All of a sudden, the horizon for Team Verstappen had changed. Before his impressive run in completely new machinery at Valencia, the question had been which Formula Renault team would they sign for? Now it was a question of which motorsport series would they aim for?

The goldfish bowl of motor-racing had taken note of Verstappen's F3 abilities and Ferrari's Luca Baldisserri was soon on the phone to Jos. A former member of the F1 race team, Baldisserri now ran the driver training programme for the Ferrari Academy. He had organized the Florida Winter Series to provide coaching for his Ferrari-signed junior drivers in cars similar to F3. He wanted to make up the numbers with drivers of similar ability, and/or the $90,000 needed to take part, such as Lance Stroll (15 at the time) and Nick Latifi, both possessing billionaire fathers.

In addition they had invited two journalists along to give the series, which would have almost no spectators, a higher profile. Ollie Marriage from *Top Gear* magazine joined the twelve together with journalist Will Buxton, now famous for his Netflix *Drive to Survive* on-screen commentary.

'It was, ostensibly, a winter training school set up by Ferrari,' Buxton recalled in an F1.com feature celebrating Max's career. 'But what was incontestably apparent was that the shining light in the group was not one of the Scuderia's own. The championship featured open data sharing after every session, and the overlays were evidence that even with his lack of experience in comparison to his fellow drivers, Max was doing things the others simply could not.'

Marriage was a bit less *Autosport* and a bit more lads' mag in his analysis. 'Ferrari invites a bunch of young karting and single-seater hot-shots and gives them all the training necessary to make it in the big, bad world of professional motorsport. Fitness, PR, racecraft, mechanics, diet – you name it, they spend a month doing it. I joined them for a few days of racing at Homestead-Miami, driving Formula-Abarth single-seaters.'

What both journalists noticed was Max's confident approach. 'Max, I quickly gathered, was the bane of the instructors' lives,' reported Marriage. 'He questioned everything, wasn't afraid to argue his point and rarely backed down. For a 16-year-old he was remarkably self-assured.'

Buxton agreed. 'He got up their (the other drivers) noses, frustrating them with his pace and raw, sometimes borderline racecraft, a trait which would create so many early headlines. He was a cut above, and everyone knew it, his consistently improving form and no-****-given approach creating a clear target on himself as the coming man.'

At first Max showed that you can take the boy out of the kart, but it's hard to take the kart out of the boy. The only racing Max had ever known was in close contact with other karts racing side by side in a pack, tucking in right behind with the occasional brush and nudge in corners. The rolling start of kart races often resembled a swarm of angry bees. He couldn't do this with the Formula Abarth cars without having to collect his front wing from somewhere out on the circuit. He had already damaged his car before even reaching the track. Pulling out into the pitlane he didn't see that Antonio Fuoco, an old karting rival now signed to the Ferrari academy, had come to a halt in front of him. Max crashed into the back of Fuoco, breaking his suspension and requiring urgent repairs.

The results across the four race events at Sebring, Palm Beach International and Homestead-Miami Speedway were mixed. There were twelve races, three per event, with Homestead used twice. For one race each week they reversed the grid and so there were eight potential poles of which Max scored three. He won two races compared to the four of Fuoco and three of Latifi, both of whom were already Prema Powerteam drivers. Prema was the race team preparing the cars for Ferrari in Florida and out on the circuit Jos, with his engine-tuning-sensitive ears, detected a difference in the engine notes of some of the cars. He was convinced

ABOVE: Max may not have swept the opposition at the FWS, but the teenager made a deep impression on journalist Will Buxton.

ABOVE RIGHT: The Abarth cars used for the FWS lined up at Sebring. Raymond Vermeulen, Max's manager, stands in front of his car, while Jos watches from the garage.

that Prema favoured their own drivers – as any competitive dad would – even though the cars should have been identical.

For *Top Gear* journalist Ollie Marriage there was only one winner: 'Ahead I saw Max draft up behind another car and send it up the inside of not just him, but another three cars in the space of as many metres. I couldn't conceive of how time, distance and physics would permit such a move, let alone the bravery, confidence and skill level needed to not only consider it, but attempt it and make it stick to perfection. I was gob-smacked.'

After the race he got talking to Jos and Huub Rothengatter, who had mostly funded the trip, and they offered him a bet that Max would be on the F1 grid by 2017. The journalist refused because, jokingly, he thought it might be sooner.

The Florida series proved to be a valuable learning experience for Max. Although the races and results had been extensively covered by the Formula Scout website, one of the most comprehensive websites for the junior formulae, Max's steep learning curve in single-seaters had been away from the public gaze. Apart from the obvious car handling and racecraft skills he had gained, he also had the experience of running behind a safety car, which would prove valuable in the F3 campaign ahead.

That's where Team Verstappen was now heading. They were going to bypass Formula Renault 2.0. Max explained the logic to fellow Red Bull driver, Estonian Yuri Vips, in a podcast. 'I was about to sign for Formula Renault two-litre and then Timo (Rumpfkeil, boss of Motopark) called my dad and Raymond and he said, "I've got two test days at Valencia with an F3 car and if you want you can drive it". We said "no, we're going to stay in two litres." And he said, "just try it".

'So we went and I loved it – it's just like a KZ kart, but in a big car. It was just when the European F3 was getting bigger and the German F3 was struggling, because I initially wanted to do the German F3 championship. Then we were very late with European F3 and most of the teams were already full.'

It was now clear that Max had the ability to handle an F3 car and the Winter Series had shown he could match up to Ferrari protégés Antonio Fuoco and Nicholas Latifi, both of whom were heading for European Formula 3 with Prema Powerteam in 2014. The problem was, as Max mentioned, time. It was late February and the opening round in Silverstone was less than two months away on 19 April. It was too late in the day to book a seat with one of the top teams and they would also need to go out and find sponsorship.

The good news was that Dutch team, Van Amersfoort Racing (VAR), still had a driver place, and they also had a wealth of Rothengatter/Verstappen history. Frits van Amersfoort was still in charge of the team which had run Jos as a 19-year-old.

'Huub was very close to us, he was one of the first drivers Frits helped many, many years ago,' Rob Niessink explained to Roger Gascoigne of Formula Scout. 'Huub was called by Frans Verstappen, the father of Jos, in the very early days when Jos was still in karting. Huub went over there to meet them and of course, what Jos did in karts was impressive, he was really successful.'

Rothengatter arranged with VAR for the then-19-year-old Jos Verstappen to do a test in October 1991 and Jos astonished everyone with his pace at Zandvoort, a circuit he'd never driven before. Max's test at Pembrey had uncanny echoes of his father's debut in racing cars. Niessink went on to become Jos's mechanic for the nine-race Benelux Formula Vauxhall-Lotus, of which Jos won eight rounds, and today is CEO of the VAR team.

Reassuringly, Frits van Amersfoort was also still in charge of operations when Jos came to see him about a 2014 drive in European Formula 3. The Dutch team

ABOVE: Max's under-sponsored car at the official European Formula 3 test in Austria.

were enthusiastic to renew the relationship and pointed out that Max would be able to give his feedback in Dutch, his first language. Max already had strong English language skills but van Amersfoort thought that explaining the minutiae of changes with his Dutch engineer Rik Vernooij in his native language would be an advantage. And the team were based in the Netherlands, which would make it very convenient for Jos to drop in...

Having found a team, the biggest hurdle came next. Finding a budget. Max already enjoyed sponsorship from the Dutch supermarket chain Jumbo, (the

sponsor of the Jumbo-Visma cycling team which dominated the Tour de France in 2022 and 2023). Team Verstappen would need to find around $800,000 in total and very quickly, too.

'For Max and the Verstappen family, it's so easy to find sponsorship now but, in the beginning, after Max and Jos agreed to start with us, we couldn't find anybody to finance the car,' Frits van Amersfoort admitted to *Autosport*. 'That's very Dutch – now they're all ready to jump on a rolling train and take the benefit from it. But in the beginning, when it's still all insecure and uncertain, they won't do it.'

Huub Rothengatter might have felt that he and Raymond Vermeulen had an extra obligation to find the money. It was Huub who had argued strongly for Max to go into the more expensive European Formula 3, whereas Jos was in favour of the less financially stressful Formula Renault series.

The logic of the Formula Renault move was that given his innate talent, Max could dominate a series and then get signed up by one of the circling F1 teams who would pay for a 2015 season in F3 or GP2. Speaking to Dutch journalist Andre Hoogeboom, Frits van Amersfoort revealed that Rothengatter was heavily invested in Max's future and would not stand by and let his career stall. 'I have to say that Huub played a very important role during this period. He not only paid for the seat in Florida, after that, on the day we signed our contracts, Huub also provided a substantial part of the budget.'

The fact that Huub and Jos fell out during the course of 2014 and ended their business relationship is a source of disappointment for van Amersfoort. 'They can both be quite assertive and have difficulty admitting anything. It's no secret that there was a bit of a row,' he told Hoogeboom, 'I have experienced that too. At the Formula 3 race in Macau the engineer was sacked by Jos. That's his character: he goes to the edge of what's permissible, but sometimes also over that edge.'

For the meantime, with contracts signed and the finances in place it was time for Max to test the car he would be driving at the first round – the Six Hours of Silverstone race weekend. By early April he was being strapped into a Dallara F312 for laps of the Red Bull Ring at Spielberg. The series he was entering was an official FIA-organized series, so testing would be restricted through the season. The European F3 races were often run as part of the high-profile DTM, the German touring car series, so time on track at race weekend was limited. This wasn't a case of pounding around a karting track until the tyres wore down to the canvas. Max would need to get on the pace with his F3 car very quickly. As he

ABOVE LEFT: Frits Van Amersfoort: Max's success with VAR doubtlessly helped them sign Mick Schumacher and Adrian Newey's son, Harrison Newey, for future series.

ABOVE RIGHT: Max looks slightly nervous as he waits to go out in F3 testing.

LEFT: Max in action at the Red Bull Ring, early August 2014.

had shown on his very first test in South Wales this would become one of his skill sets. Max loved the car and felt he could do a lot more with it than he could with a Formula Renault.

In recent years the Red Bull Ring has become a second home grand prix thanks to the Oranje Army of Verstappen supporters who turn up to watch him race. Right from the start it has been a circuit on which he excels. In the FIA-organized test there, without having driven the track before, he was two-tenths of a second clear of a field that included Esteban Ocon, Antonio Fuoco, Jake Dennis, Nicholas Latifi, Antonio Giovinazzi and Tatania Calderón – many of whom he'd raced in Florida. This time, with strict FIA scrutineering in place, there could be no preferential engine tuning. He was a whole second clear of team-mate Gustavo Menezes on what is a reasonably short lap – the shorter the lap, the more impressive the gap.

At Silverstone, the first weekend of the season, a clutch problem eliminated him from Race 1, and a slow start in Race 2 dropped him back to eighth place from where he recovered to fifth. It was the final race of the weekend where his growing Dutch fanbase got to see his real potential, slotting into third place from the start behind Fuoco and Ocon. While Fuoco disappeared into the distance, Max engaged battle with Ocon.

ABOVE: Max shadows series rival, Prema team driver Esteban Ocon, at Silverstone.

ABOVE RIGHT: Jos poses with Max at the Hungaroring test in April. Hard to believe, but in six months' time he would be sat in an F1 car at Suzuka.

Each lap behind the Frenchman was a lesson in the art of following another car, managing the loss of downforce while keeping the tyres in shape and looking for an opportunity to pass. Silverstone is a wide track with a good mixture of curves, but the Dutchman couldn't find a way past despite being just a second back for over five laps. Eventually he pressured Ocon into a braking error and Max was through, but the battle had let Fuoco escape up the road and he was forced to settle for second place.

A podium on his first racing weekend in F3 was not a shabby return. Jos enjoyed bigging up his son's achievement in his column for *De Telegraaf* and confessed that Max was much further down the road than he'd anticipated. And the publicity would surely bring more sponsors on board.

Two weeks later at Hockenheim Max managed his first win of the campaign, but again he had to wait until Race 3 to put in his best performance.

The first race had ended in disaster after a shunt of his own making. Blocked off the startline by a slow-starting Giovinazzi, Max lost two places and was anxious to get them back. The hairpin at Hockenheim follows a long, slightly curving straight but demands a big stop from the driver. In his efforts to put in a demon overtaking move, not unlike the one described by *Top Gear* in Florida, Max outbraked himself and went sailing out of control into Nicholas Latifi's Prema car. Max apologized to Latifi for ruining both their races and admitted it was: '...one of my big learning moments. As you get more experience and you have more feeling about where to brake and what you have to do in the first few laps – you can't brake as late as you can do in the later laps. So you have to be more patient. In go-karts, if you touch a bit, nothing bad happens, but in F3, you'll bend something or the wing is off. So that was a lesson.'

Race 2 at Hockenheim didn't auger well for Max either. He had put his car on pole and then had to retire with a problem on the way to the grid. For Race 3 he was also on pole, but this time there would be no mistakes. *Autosport*, motor-racing's industry bible, reported that: 'The 16-year-old Dutchman became the youngest driver ever to win a race in the series in just his sixth weekend in car racing, after four "warm-up" events in the Florida Winter Series earlier this year. The win for Verstappen's Dallara-Volkswagen was also the first for the Dutch Van Amersfoort Racing team in European F3.'

Leading away from the line, Max had built up a 1.6-second advantage over Esteban Ocon, but after two laps that was cancelled out by a safety car. With the experience of safety car re-starts in Florida, Max handled it well, shadowed by Ocon to the flag.

The next two race weekends brought a poor haul of points for Team Verstappen. Max proved unfazed by the proximity of the walls at the narrow,

BELOW: Jos Verstappen awaits the arrival of Max in the Hockenheim pitlane. Next to him is his friend, photographer Frits van Eldik and Max's race engineer Rik Vernooij. Sophie Kumpen is beyond.

BELOW RIGHT: What they've been waiting for: Max has just won his first FIA single-seater race in Round 6.

Monaco-like street circuit of Pau in southern France and finished third in Race 1. There was then a duel between series leader Ocon and Max for pole position for the two Sunday races. To the delight of the home crowd Esteban edged Max out by 0.057 seconds for Race 2.

Sunday's Race 2 was wet, with a safety car start. When the race was flagged green, Max dropped back to third place then spun backwards into the tyre wall at the exit of the Foch chicane on Lap 11. Race over. For the final race Max tangled with the slow-to-get-away Ocon, who rushed across to defend his position and squeezed him against the inside barriers, clipping his front wing, an incident which dropped Max down to sixth place. Then on the second lap Max crashed out at the second chicane, so again, *nul pointes*.

Ocon was unaffected and finished second in the race and was now the runaway championship leader. Max was livid that he hadn't been left enough room for the corner. It wouldn't be the first time the two would swap paintwork on a race track.

It hardly got better in Hungary. Esteban Ocon continued to steal Max Verstappen's motorsport media thunder by making it a clean sweep of poles for all three races. Like Max, this was his rookie season in F3, unlike Max he had already

been signed up for the Lotus F1 team's junior programme and already had a season's experience of racing in Formula Renault. Max retired from the first race with mechanical issues, and in the second race he repeatedly went over track limits at Turn 4 and was given a drive-through penalty which dropped him from fifth place to 16th. He managed a fourth place in the final race, which was red-flagged after the light rain became heavy rain, just when it was getting into Verstappen territory.

As the teams headed for everyone's favourite race track at Spa-Francorchamps, Esteban Ocon held a commanding lead in the series with 232 points. Max was down in fifth place with 80. Max was doing all right for a rookie in his first season of car racing, but as we know, the Verstappens don't do 'all right'. At Spa, everything came good in the most spectacular fashion.

Max won the first two races, starting both from P2 on the grid. The first time he dragged past polesitter Ocon up the Kemmel Straight and had the satisfaction of watching Ocon tag his Prema team-mate Fuoco in his rearview mirrors and exit the race. The second time he got the better of his American team-mate Menezes who had scored a surprise pole. The strength of the Van Amersfoort Racing set-up at Spa was clear, but the third race would be more tricky as he was starting from fifth.

As the lights went out the Spa debutant squeezed down the inside of second-row starters Felix Serralles and Felipe Guimaraes to take third at the La Source hairpin. Ahead of him John Bryant-Meisner passed poleman Esteban Ocon around the outside at Les Combes to take the lead. He wouldn't keep it for very long.

LEFT: Max trails Mitch Gilbert at the start of a European F3 race in Pau.

ABOVE RIGHT: Max makes it a clean sweep – three wins out of three at Spa-Francorchamps. He is followed home by Esteban Ocon.

On the second lap, Verstappen drafted Ocon and Bryant-Meisner in one move along the Kemmel Straight to catapult from third to first at the right-hander, Les Combes. He hadn't shaken off Ocon, though. He could open a gap in the twisty middle sector of the circuit and the Prema driver would close up in the first and third. Twice he passed Verstappen on the Kemmel, slipstreaming his way past Max, and twice was repassed by him – once on the outside and once on the inside. Max had to negotiate his way through a safety car period, which closed the pack and made him vulnerable to slipstreaming up the Kemmel Straight, but he held on. Three wins on the trot.

Next up was the Norisring in Nuremberg, where he was able to demonstrate his mastery of car control in wet conditions. It was a performance that cemented his place in the Red Bull programme (see Greatest Races page 50).

THE RACE

EUROPEAN FORMULA 3
Round 6
Norisring, Germany
Races: 1, 2 & 3 – 28 and 29 June 2014

Though it sounds like it should be a permanent race facility, the Norisring is actually a street circuit in Nuremberg, Germany. It is visited by the mighty German touring car series, the DTM, once a year with Formula 3 support races. The European Formula 3 series run three races on the Saturday and Sunday, which in 2014 was part of an 11-round series of races run across the summer months.

Max's campaign had got off to a poor start, failing to record a result six times in the first ten races. Leading the series was future F1 driver Esteban Ocon in the powerful Prema team. Ocon had competed against Verstappen in karts but graduated to single-seaters two years earlier and had the experience of racing Formula Renault 2.0 (the level Max decided to skip) for two seasons before switching to Formula 3. Max was also vying with Tom Blomqvist, son of rally driver Stig Blomqvist, and Jake Dennis, who would go on to win Formula E in 2023.

The teams arrived at the Norisring on the back of the Belgian round in Spa-Francorchamps where, despite Ocon setting pole position for two of the three races, it was Verstappen who had won all three. Spa with its fearsome Eau Rouge corner and equally testing, flat-out Blanchimont curve has long been known as a benchmark circuit for motor-racing talent. Go fast at Spa and people took note. It was where Michael Schumacher had made a remarkable debut for the mid-grid Jordan team in 1991. Verstappen won all three races at Spa, a feat that moved him closer to second place in the championship and focused the attention of Red Bull's motorsport advisor, Dr Helmut Marko.

Like the diligent professor he resembles, Marko had been following Verstappen's results from the start of the series and Max's

RIGHT: Max leads in the dry at the Norisring, but it was his wet weather driving that made him stand out.

BELOW: Esteban Ocon, Max and Jake Dennis share a podium at the Norisring. Jake now drives in Formula E and also puts in time on the Red Bull simulator.

performance at the Norisring convinced him that he needed to move quickly to sign him to the Red Bull programme. Verstappen won the Saturday race in the dry, but it was the rain that fell on Sunday which marked out the Dutchman's advantage over the rest of the field. 'The moment I thought he was really special was at the Norisring,' Marko revealed later; 'it was more wet than dry and he was over two seconds per lap faster than anyone else.'

What marked out Verstappen's win even further was his ability to control the race after a number of safety car re-starts had closed up the field. When he took the chequered flag for the final race of the weekend he had won six races in a row, three in Belgium, three in Germany, something that had never been achieved in European F3. Only the first race had seen the demon overtaking moves trademarked by Verstappen at Spa, but the manner of his victories, especially when taken in context with the Belgian circuit, had shown what a compelling and comprehensive talent he was in his first season of single-seaters. At 16.

F1 ROOKIE

inning six races in a row at the Norisring was as good as it got in European Formula 3 for Max Verstappen in 2014. Or perhaps, winning seven races in a row if you include his Masters of Formula 3 one-off race at Zandvoort, before the championship reconvened at the Moscow Raceway.

The Masters has a special place in Dutch motorsport history. Back in 1993, when it was known as the Marlboro Masters, Jos Verstappen had just won the German Formula 3 series with one race to go and looked destined for a career in F1. Helped by a publicity campaign organized by Huub Rothengatter and backed by Marlboro money, a crowd of 56,000 Dutch fans had turned up at Zandvoort to watch an F3 race, a staggering number. The fact that it was free entry helped, but it showed there could be enormous support for a successful Dutch driver. Jos duly delivered a win for the Van Amersfoort team, taking a lights-to-flag victory.

When Max Verstappen took the chequered flag at Zandvoort for the Masters of Formula 3, there was a smaller crowd in attendance to see son emulate father. Max had actually stepped out of the Van Amersfoort team for this non-championship event and was driving for team Motopark. It had been Motopark boss Timo Rumpfkeil who had offered Max the two-day test in Valencia less than a year earlier which had been so important in his switch up to Formula 3.

Verstappen Junior paid him back with interest; the win at Zandvoort was the 200th victory for Rumpfkeil's team. The 16-year-old had also become the youngest driver to win the Masters Formula 3 event. It was the kind of statistic Max was going to have to get used to.

PREVIOUS PAGE: Max pulls out of the Toro Rosso garage.

LEFT: All Red Bulled up: Max poses beside his European F3 Dallara tricked out in its new Red Bull livery for the remaining races of the season.

Esteban Ocon wasted no time in reinforcing his lead at the top of the European Formula 3 championship by winning all three races at the next round in Moscow, but the spotlight had already drifted away. Max was now the driver everyone was talking about. He managed two podiums and a retirement in Moscow. Not bad, but not good enough to maintain a championship challenge when consistency scores much higher than wins and DNFs.

Max would go on to win again at the Nürburgring, Imola and Hockenheim, but he would fail to finish in one race at the Nürburgring and one race at Imola, and the impetus was gone. By season's end, the paint scheme on Max Verstappen's Van Amersfoort Dallara F312 looked considerably different to how it had appeared during the test session in Austria. And Max Verstappen's race suit had a similar Red Bull livery.

ABOVE LEFT: Max on the podium alongside future F1 driver Antonio Giovinazzi and VAR engineering chief Rob Niessink.

ABOVE: Max retires his car after Race 2 at the Nürburgring, with any chance of a series win gone.

HELMUT MARKO

Helmut Marko had been in touch with the Verstappens during his karting career. Like Eric Boullier he was a driver talent scout, but Marko was the most important driver scout bar none. Luca Baldisserri at Ferrari might have had the marque, but Marko had the money. When it came to seeding money into the lower formulae of motorsport, the Red Bull organization were unmatched in their investment, from karting all the way through to Formula 1. Red Bull not only gave you wings, they gave you slicks.

'I usually like to talk to a driver for about twenty minutes to get a picture of his personality, but with Max I sat for an hour and a half. He was a young body with a mind that was certainly three to five years ahead,' Marko revealed to German tabloid newspaper *Bild* in 2016. 'Now his development has slowly levelled off and his age and his maturity have come together. And it is far above average.'

Even though Verstappen had made an impression on Marko during his time in karts, it had not been enough to convince the Austrian to invest early in Max's career. One glance at a podium photo of a Euro Series KF3 karting event in South Garda, Italy, from March 2010 shows a beaming Alex Albon resplendent in Red Bull overalls on the top step, with Max in his factory-CRG overalls on a lower step.

There was also a strong element of Jos wanting to keep control. If Max was signed up to a driver programme then the finances may have been easier, but he would lose the ability to shape his son's career.

Helmut Marko had reached his position of absolute authority in the Red Bull organization through his friendship with fellow Austrian, Red Bull boss, Dietrich 'Didi' Mateschitz. Helmut had grown up with school friend Jochen Rindt, F1's only posthumous champion, and together they visited race tracks across Europe with Rindt getting his first serious F1 drive for Cooper in 1965. Marko completed his legal doctorate

RIGHT: Helmut at the wheel of the mighty Porsche 917K on his way to winning Le Mans in 1971.

BELOW: Marko's Formula 1 career was cut painfully short by an accident at the French Grand Prix.

before racing at Le Mans in a Porsche 908, finishing third overall in 1970 and winning in a Porsche 917 in 1971, alongside Dutch driver Gijs van Lennep.

Rindt was a driver with spectacular style, very much in the mould of Jos and Max Verstappen, but Marko was no slouch himself. He still holds the lap record for the fearsomely dangerous Targa Florio road race in Italy (before it was banned) and was just two seasons into his F1 career racing a BRM when tragedy struck.

The French Grand Prix of 1972 was held at the Charade circuit near Clermont-Ferrand. Charade winds up and down and round the base of an extinct volcano, with the track jammed up against the mountainside in many places, with little run-off and rocks occasionally falling onto the circuit. During the 1972 French Grand Prix ten drivers, suffered tyre punctures and those who put a wheel over the

track edge often sent jagged stones flying back onto the racing line.

Early in the race a stone pierced Helmut Marko's visor, blinding him in one eye. The Austrian managed to steer his car, still laden with 250 litres of high octane fuel, to safety before he passed out with pain. Just getting the car stopped without it ending in a fireball was a considerable feat.

His career as a driver was over, but he would go on to manage Austrian drivers Gerhard Berger and Karl Wendlinger, before setting up his own F3000 team (the forerunner to F2). Dietrich Mateschitz was a big Formula 1 fan and had followed Marko's career, so when he decided to promote the Red Bull drinks brand through motorsport, it was Helmut he turned to.

Apart from managing the sponsorship of the Sauber team, Helmut devised the Red Bull junior programme, and most significantly of all, recruited Christian Horner to run the Red Bull team. He first met Christian in Calais while selling him an F3000 trailer. The Red Bull team was set up when the drinks firm ended their deal with Sauber. Mateschitz had bought the Jaguar team and severed ties with

ABOVE: Celebrating Max's second world championship with Adrian Newey in Japan, 2022.

ABOVE RIGHT: Helmut talks to Max on the grid just before his breakthrough race in 2015, the Malaysian Grand Prix.

Sauber because Peter Sauber refused to take Red Bull protégé Enrique Bernoldi, preferring some Finnish kid called Kimi Räikkönen.

Marko's Red Bull Junior programme had yielded the incomparable Sebastian Vettel and paddock favourite Daniel Ricciardo, but there had been slip-ups too. American Red Bull driver Scott Speed had a volatile relationship with Franz Tost, Austrian boss of the Toro Rosso team, and been sacked mid-season after a frank exchange of views. Halfway through the 2009 season the team sacked Sébastien Bourdais for 'not meeting expectations' i.e. 'not beating his inexperienced team-mate' and Jaime Alguersuari was parachuted into the team.

At the 2009 Hungarian Grand Prix in August, Alguersuari became the youngest ever Formula 1 driver at the age of 19 years and 125 days, breaking the record previously held by New Zealander Mike Thackwell. He was only the seventh teenager to start a Formula 1 grand prix. He had little success in his first season, his best result coming at the 2009 Brazilian Grand Prix where he managed 14th place.

Along the way he wrecked his STR4 in spectacular fashion at Suzuka's flat-out 130R curve. His second season was hardly better, scraping two ninth places. It was only in his final year that he started to show promise with seventh- and eighth-place finishes but by then Helmut had run out of patience. At season end both Toro Rosso drivers were replaced with new arrivals Daniel Ricciardo and Jean-Eric Vergne for 2012.

Alguersuari's driving career was effectively over at 21. The F1 paddock saw it as a case of Marko promoting a driver far too early, and then Red Bull spitting him out when he had not become the 'new Sebastian Vettel'. These were exactly the fears that surfaced when Max Verstappen was announced as a Red Bull-contracted driver. First his father was put into a top team before he'd learned the sport; now the same thing was going to happen to his son.

Toto Recall

Helmut Marko and the Red Bull team were not the only major player keen to get Max's signature after his stand-out Formula 3 performances. Mercedes were in contact with Team Verstappen and represented a real opportunity for the future. In 2014, the first season of the new hybrid engine regulations, they had produced the fastest car which would take Lewis Hamilton to his second world championship. Red Bull had fallen from multiple series winner into the pack of Mercedes' pursuers and Christian Horner was fuming at the lack of progress from Renault, their engine supplier. That made the Silver Arrows an interesting proposition.

'I spoke to Jos and Huub when they came to my office in Brackley (Mercedes HQ) and that must have been when Max was in karting or the end of his karting days just before Formula 3,' Toto Wolff told ESPN. 'And then we spoke again when Max and Jos visited me in my house in Vienna. We spent a few hours discussing his future.'

At that time Mercedes didn't have a junior team they could offer Verstappen a seat in. By far a more conservative outfit than Red Bull, Wolff wanted to see the progress Max could make in GP2, the formula just below F1 that was replaced by Formula 2 for the 2017 season.

BELOW: Toto Wolff chats with Max as they walk through the F1 paddock in 2015.

'We had two drivers that I was extremely happy with, in Nico and Lewis, and when Nico left, Valtteri was then the option and Max wasn't even available.'

What may have affected Wolff's judgement in the matter was that Valtteri Bottas was one of his own managed drivers. Had he known that Nico Rosberg was going to shock the F1 world and announce his retirement directly after the 2016 season he might have had a different view on the Silver Arrows' succession plan. But he denies that he missed a golden opportunity.

'Back in the day there wasn't huge hype around Max, because Max and Van Amersfoort weren't winning the championship that year,' is Wolff's retrospective view. 'Esteban won in a more competitive car. So the insiders knew that Max probably was in an inferior package and in his first year, and the insiders knew there was a very good driver coming, but it wasn't clear that he was that good at that stage.

'You can only say when someone grows in F1, and matures, that he is a true world champion – an outstanding one. Before we had Lewis, and then Michael Schumacher, and before that Senna. Who is the next one? Was it clear that Max would step into these shoes? It wasn't clear back then. Do I regret missing out on Max? Certainly. But it wasn't an option back in the day.'

Speechless

Wolff may have had his doubts, but Marko was positive that Max Verstappen would be a perfect fit for the Red Bull stable. He was young, fast, exciting to watch, he had a famous F1 father, spoke perfect English, no matter that he was 17. As long as he could put in the mileage to obtain a superlicence things would be fine.

Before he did anything he contacted Franz Tost, who would be responsible for managing his early seasons in F1 at Toro Rosso, and the two Austrians reviewed his results. Marko had been watching all his European Formula 3 races that year and kept Franz in the loop. Tost was positive. Marko was free to offer.

Interviewed for the documentary *Whatever It Takes* Helmut pinpoints the moment he knew he had to get Max's name on a contract. His answer reveals that, like Wolff, they had been putting forward the idea to Jos that they would sponsor Max for a year in a lower formula.

'It was after this famous race at the Norisring, Max was in a class on his own and that impressed me massively and convinced me – we were talking about Formula 2/GP2 – and I had the opinion we don't need all of that. So I called Jos in the morning and said, "Forget all that, we do Formula 1."

'The line went quiet for about a minute and I said, "Jos... Jos... Jos...?"'

Marko is notorious for calling people early in the morning, so for a minute he thought that Verstappen Senior wasn't fully listening. It was the Monday morning after the Norisring race on Sunday and there had been a long, 500km journey home and a late night for Max and Jos. It all seemed too good to be true.

When Jos phoned Sophie with the news that 'Red Bull want Max' she was convinced her ex-husband was winding her up. He assured her it was true. With Max still a legal minor at 16, Jos would need to involve and include Sophie every step of the way. The good news was that with Raymond Vermeulen overseeing the contracts, a man trusted by both partners, there were likely to be few bumps in the road.

Jos, Raymond and Max flew to Graz in Austria to finalize the details of the contract. Max would be signing for Toro Rosso for two years, with options. At first he would be announced as signed to the Red Bull Junior programme, so the Van Amersfoort F3 car would be decked out in the Red Bull livery for the remaining three race weekends of the European Formula 3 season, starting with the Nürburgring on 15 August.

Then, once that information had filtered through the motorsport media, they would announce that Van Amersfoort would be taking Max to the prestigious Macau F3 race.

After that would come the F1 announcement – there were still a lot of races on the calendar and the news would certainly unsettle the existing Toro Rosso drivers. But before they could execute that media plan... the news got out.

On 13 August, a 'source' within the team leaked the news to *De Telegraaf* newspaper that Max would be joining Toro Rosso in 2015. As it turned out, the final contract had yet to be signed. Five days later though, with two Verstappens and one Kumpen signature on a legal document, Red Bull could announce their coup.

'We are happy to welcome Max into the Toro Rosso family,' Franz Tost said in the stilted official speak of the team press release. 'It's great to see how the Red Bull Junior Programme continues to find talented young drivers and gives them the opportunity to come into Formula 1. We consider Max to be one of the most skilled young drivers of the new generation and we believe he has the necessary maturity and mental strength to take on this challenge successfully.'

Jos revealed to F1's post-race interviewer Tom Clarkson in his Beyond the Grid podcast how it had all panned out: 'Helmut offered us a seat with Toro Rosso. It's so difficult to get into Formula 1, so when he offered that I said: "Okay, but we

F1 DRIVER RESULTS AT THE AGE OF 26

Max turned 26 on September 30th 2023, having already completed 100 more races than Lewis Hamilton at that age.

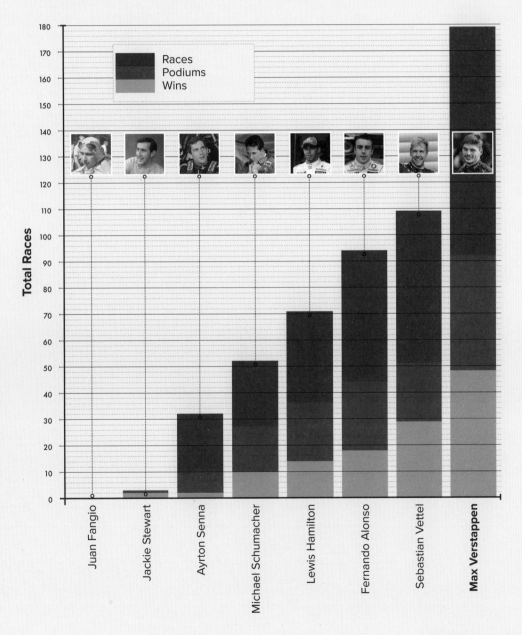

Legend:
- Races
- Podiums
- Wins

Y-axis: Total Races (0 to 180)

Drivers:
- Juan Fangio
- Jackie Stewart
- Ayrton Senna
- Michael Schumacher
- Lewis Hamilton
- Fernando Alonso
- Sebastian Vettel
- Max Verstappen

don't do it for one year, we do it for two years. First year we learn and we do a proper job."'

News of Max's great leap forward wasn't universally welcomed in F1, and there were a lot of envious competitors in European Formula 3. 'Well done to him, definitely, but when I saw the news it was difficult to swallow,' Esteban Ocon admitted. 'He was third in the championship; I was winning, and I didn't have a seat in any category at that time. I'd done a few tests in GP2, but there was nothing really confirmed. The Lotus F1 junior programme had problems at the time and I wasn't going anywhere, so it was quite a challenging moment.'

Jaime Alguersuari and Daniil Kvyat had been Red Bull's previous two 'youngest

DRIVER HEIGHTS AND WEIGHTS

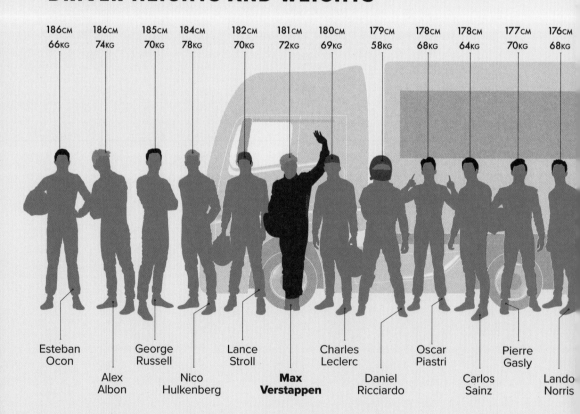

| 186cm | 186cm | 185cm | 184cm | 182cm | 181cm | 180cm | 179cm | 178cm | 178cm | 177cm | 176cm |
| 66kg | 74kg | 70kg | 78kg | 70kg | 72kg | 69kg | 58kg | 68kg | 64kg | 70kg | 68kg |

Esteban Ocon

Alex Albon

George Russell

Nico Hulkenberg

Lance Stroll

Max Verstappen

Charles Leclerc

Daniel Ricciardo

Oscar Piastri

Carlos Sainz

Pierre Gasly

Lando Norris

drivers on the grid' and armed with Max's birthdate of 30 September calculations were made about how Verstappen would easily lower that benchmark in Melbourne in 2015.

The great and the good of Formula 1 weighed in with their views. Not surprisingly, ex-Red Bull driver David Coulthard was supportive. 'I'm a great believer if you're good enough you're old enough. Sport has shown us many times that age is no barrier to delivering results.'

Coulthard was racing when the 21-year-old Kimi Räikkönen made his debut for Sauber in 2001. Räikkönen may have been four years older than Max, but in terms of experience he had driven only 23 Formula Renault races – winning 13 of

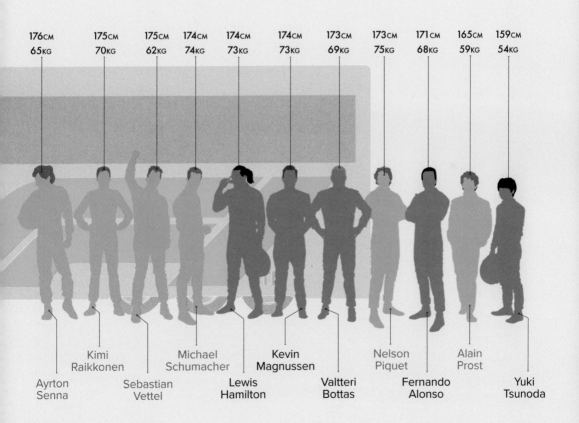

| 176CM | 175CM | 175CM | 174CM | 174CM | 174CM | 173CM | 173CM | 171CM | 165CM | 159CM |
| 65KG | 70KG | 62KG | 74KG | 73KG | 73KG | 69KG | 75KG | 68KG | 59KG | 54KG |

Ayrton Senna · Kimi Raikkonen · Sebastian Vettel · Michael Schumacher · Lewis Hamilton · Kevin Magnussen · Valtteri Bottas · Nelson Piquet · Fernando Alonso · Alain Prost · Yuki Tsunoda

them. Peter Sauber was confident that his Finnish rookie would have no problems adapting to Formula 1, but FIA President, Max Mosley, wasn't convinced.

Räikkönen was handed a four-race probation period, after which he would get his superlicence. Kimi drove a competent race in Australia (in the 2000s, Sauber were very good at starting their seasons with a reliable package) and scored points on his debut. By the fourth race no-one was questioning his ability.

In comparison, Max Verstappen's racing record would be 47 races – 12 in Florida, 33 in European Formula 3, plus the Masters at Zandvoort and the Macau F3 event. He hadn't grown up in rural Espoo, Finland, he had spent his life visiting Formula 1 races with his father and was fully attuned to the hustle, bustle and buzz of a grand prix weekend. He'd been to the Belgian Grand Prix before with his father, now the news was out, he could attend the next grand prix, which just happened to be nearby at Spa-Francorchamps. It was the chance to meet people in the Toro Rosso team, but it was also the chance to show his face to the sceptical media.

Rarely mentioned at the time was that since Kimi Räikkönen had made his debut, simulator technology had made quantum leaps forward. 'New joiners' to the F1 grid could pound round every track on the grand prix calendar with a realistic feel for how their car would behave. They would be fully prepared when

the time came. In 2023, when the Alpha Tauri team (Toro Rosso that was) had to replace Daniel Ricciardo in a hurry after he broke his hand at Zandvoort, Liam Lawson stepped in for his first grand prix weekend and produced notable results without ever testing the car.

That didn't stop the prophets of doom from having their say. Double world champion Mika Häkkinen was negative. 'It's too young because in F1, the risk is high. In Formula 1 you don't go to learn, you have to be ready. F1 doesn't allow you to do too much learning.'

Canadian world champion Jacques Villeneuve was similarly dubious and employed a questionable analogy. 'He is still a boy so it is very risky. You don't take a 16-year-old, who hasn't even been to university, in the best hospital as a doctor, even if he is very good and very intelligent. You need to pay dues; you need to deserve it because that is only how you will become a man.'

It's very likely that neither of them had fully appreciated Max's performances in European Formula 3, simply looked at his age and reacted. Jean Todt was President of the FIA at the time and like his predecessor commented: 'For me personally, I think it's too young.' But then again, he had to say that. The idea that a 17-year-old could reach the pinnacle of motorsport negated the role of the many junior formulae he and the FIA were responsible for.

BELOW LEFT: Sixteen-year-old Max Verstappen fearlessly engages with the media in the Spa paddock, 21 August, 2014.

BELOW: Raymond, Max and Jos watch activity in the Toro Rosso garage during the 2014 Belgian GP.

What would be the point of having Formula Ford, Formula Renault, F4, F3 and F2 if you could spend one season in European Formula 3 and get taken on by a top F1 team? Almost all the young racers in the lower categories had ambitions of making it to Formula 1 one day. Without that constant supply of young hopefuls, many of the series would wither and die.

Other drivers were welcoming. Fernando Alonso offered some Zen-like advice. 'Some people are ready at 17, some people are ready at 28 – that is what we don't know. So before saying anything we need to see how Verstappen does next year

and after six to eight races we can see if he was ready or not. But at the moment anyone is ready.'

Nico Rosberg was equally positive: 'Journalists are always asking, "Is it only with money that you can get to Formula 1?" and things like that. It's great to see that if you have the talent and you really deserve it, you can get there.'

Helmut Marko's reaction to the criticism was suitably Helmut: 'When it was public that he was going to be in an F1 car it was unbelievable. The Dutch people went crazy, but a lot of the others said, no, you can't do it, it's dangerous and blah blah blah – but that is just jealousy.'

In a feature for Formula 1.com, veteran F1 journalist David Tremayne recalled how he'd bumped into Jos and Max when they visited the Spa-Francorchamps circuit for the Belgian Grand Prix, just after the Toro Rosso drive had been announced.

'I'd always got on well with Jos, and waited until the crush had disappeared before being introduced to his boy. When he'd arrived in the world two days after his dad raced at Tyrrell in the 1997 Luxembourg GP, Joe Saward (fellow F1 journalist) and I had said that if he ever raced, with a dad like Jos and karting star mum Sophie Kumpen, Max would be a star. We'd both felt smug that weekend, and I may have mentioned our incredible foresight to him... I remember the most impressive thing about Max even then was how he let all the fuss go straight over his head. He couldn't have cared less what Jacques (Villeneuve) thought and was completely unruffled by it. Not a lot has changed, has it?'

Max's early confirmation for Toro Rosso in 2015 inevitably meant that one of its current drivers would be leaving. Jean-Eric Vergne had been driving for Franz Tost for three years in 2014 and as a general rule three years in a Red Bull organization car is enough for Helmut. Sébastien Buemi and Jaime Alguersuari had been given three years before being dropped, so the writing was on the wall. Jean-Eric, or 'JEV' as he's affectionately known, got the call earlier than he'd expected in his final season.

'In the summer I was called and told that I would be replaced by a younger driver. I knew that would be Max Verstappen,' recalls the Frenchman who has since gone on to become a double Formula E world champion. 'That's just how the game works, there was no more room (for promotion to) Red Bull Racing. I hadn't spoken to any other F1 team because I belonged to the Red Bull family, that was maybe a mistake on my part.'

What Jean-Eric regrets most of all was the early announcement of his replacement. In the last half of the 2014 season he outperformed his Toro Rosso team-mate Daniil Kvyat, scoring points in three of the last six races and finishing the year with 22 points compared to Kvyat's 8 points.

Nobody had expected Sebastian Vettel to leave Red Bull and when he made his blindsiding announcement of a move to Ferrari in October (very much like his shock retirement from Aston Martin in 2022) it was Kvyat who was promoted to the senior team.

Results from the races beyond August pointed to JEV as being a far more worthy candidate for a seat alongside Daniel Ricciardo, who he'd often matched when they were team-mates. Pitlane cynics pointed out that there was a much bigger market for Red Bull drinks in Russia than there was in France. Also, Jean-Eric had an extra motivation to show other teams his potential and Helmut Marko that he'd got it wrong.

Still, Vettel's departure gave Vergne a potential lifeline and in October, Red Bull announced they were weighing up a shortlist of Vergne and Red Bull juniors Carlos Sainz, Pierre Gasly and Alex Lynn to be Verstappen's team-mate.

Asked by journalists who he'd like in the other car, Max sided with Jean-Eric. 'He has experience with the tyres already so he can help me a lot with that. If you have someone like Jean-Eric for sure they will help – not only for one race but I think the whole season. I think it is a win-win situation for me and the team.'

MODERN DUTCH F1 DRIVERS

The name Verstappen dominates Dutch motorsport. Max had completed more
Formula 1 races at 22, than father Jos in his career.

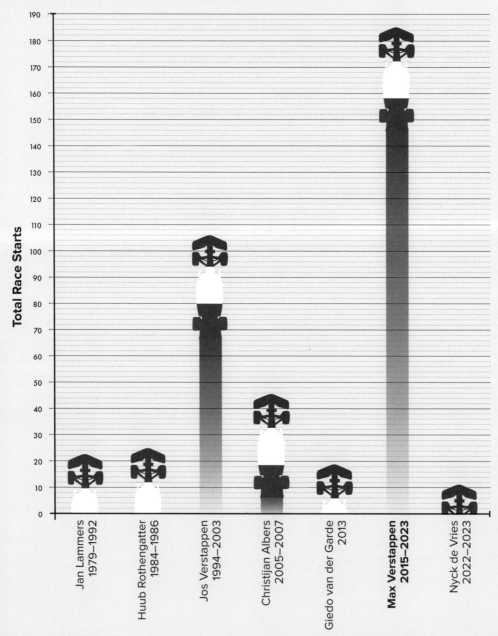

Total Race Starts

Jan Lammers
1979–1992

Huub Rothengatter
1984–1986

Jos Verstappen
1994–2003

Christijan Albers
2005–2007

Giedo van der Garde
2013

**Max Verstappen
2015–2023**

Nyck de Vries
2022–2023

JEV had been on hand to help him through his first grand prix weekend at Suzuka in early October. That was after a whirlwind few weeks in late August and September that involved seat fittings, media events, the European Formula 3 season and a visit to Rockingham Speedway to spend time in an old Toro Rosso to get him used to the sheer speed of the car he was stepping into. Once he had mastered the multi-functional array of knobs and dials that is the modern F1 steering wheel he was set loose on the streets of Rotterdam.

Long before there was a sniff of an F1 drive, one of his sponsors, car leasing firm VKV, had booked him for a demonstration run as part of their VKV City Racing event. In the past, Max had bounced along the city streets in one of his karts, now Red Bull allowed him to drive the current Toro Rosso through the streets of the Dutch port city.

Thousands of fans turned up to watch his three-lap demonstration run, haring along city streets, with a wide square to throw in some donuts. Kimi Räikkönen was there too at the wheel of the Ferrari F60 from 2009 with its old-school V8 engine screaming a lot louder than the modern hybrid engine. Unfortunately for Max, the steering rack on the Toro Rosso wasn't set up for tight, Monaco-like turns and in trying to get some speed up to turn the car round he simply lumped it into the barriers, removing the front wing.

It wasn't a great omen for what might happen at Suzuka. As TopGear.com noted next to a video of the event: 'For most young drivers, three-point-turning your parents' Vauxhall Corsa around Sainsbury's car park in Neasden is about as stressful as it gets. If you happen to be 16-year-old Dutch wunderkind Max Verstappen, the learning curve is somewhat steeper.'

Once Max had finished 300km of running in an F1 car at the Adria Raceway, north of the Toro Rosso base at Faenza, Italy, he received his superlicence to drive in F1. Franz Tost had supervised 150 flawless laps of the 2km circuit and was convinced he was ready.

It had been an emotional moment for Jos. 'We got there. His name was on the car. It was sensational. He was sixteen, a child, in a Formula 1 car.'

The team were then free to announce on 30 September that he would be taking part in his first grand prix weekend at the 2014 Japanese Grand Prix, racing in Free Practice 1.

The first practice session of an F1 weekend is usually the least significant of all the time spent out on track. It gives teams time to shake down the car, get a general feel for the tarmac and kerbs (sometimes they get modified between grands prix) and if the car set-up is as they anticipated. No heroics or banzai laps are completed in FP1. The track is yet to rubber in, with grip steadily increasing over the course of a race weekend. With engine longevity now a firm part of the hybrid era, engine modes are switched to conservative.

Some teams will run old engines. Any driver who dumps their car in the wall in Free Practice 1 is severely hampering the team's progress for the whole weekend. Having seen a rookie driver knock off a new front wing, race engineers may ask over team radio, 'Are you okay?' when really they want to ask the Enzo Ferrari question – 'Is the car okay?'

The Suzuka circuit, owned by Honda, is an old-school Formula 1 track designed by the same man responsible for the original Zandvoort, John Hugenholtz. In places it has very little run-off, especially Degner 2, the downhill

ABOVE: Jos with Max as he prepares for his Toro Rosso FP1 debut at Suzuka.

ABOVE RIGHT: 'Back to the day job', European F3 at the Variante Alta, Imola.

RIGHT: Bringing the Toro Rosso STR9 back to the garage at Suzuka in one piece.

FAR RIGHT: Max and JEV listen as engineer Xevi Pujolar talks with team boss Franz Tost in Suzuka.

right-hander just before the track passes under itself, Suzuka being the only figure-of-eight circuit on the calendar. There is gravel on the outside of many of the corners, so FP1 rookies beware. Plant your car in the shingle early on and bumping off your front wing in a Rotterdam demonstration run would pale into insignificance.

No pressure then.

With the announcement that Max would replace Jean-Eric Vergne for FP1, the media buzz that greeted his drive for 2015 reignited. The record books would need to be adjusted: at 17 years and three days Max would become the youngest driver to take part in a grand prix weekend. And he would stay the youngest. Alarmed that his arrival on the grid might open the door to more inexperienced teenagers taking that route, the FIA took action. Some struggling teams at the back of the grid would often help their finances by offering an FP1 session to wealthy drivers with superlicences, so tightening the criteria for getting one wasn't entirely aimed at Max.

It was too late to bolt the stable door for 2015, but from 2016 superlicence applicants would need to be at least eighteen years old and have at least two

ABOVE: Max is fitted into his Toro Rosso seat at Suzuka and adjusts to the new cockpit and a far more sophisticated steering wheel.

years of racing in single-seaters. There would be a points scheme, where success in a higher series, such as F2, would count for more than a lower series.

While many were half-expecting a needless dink or an off-track excursion at Suzuka, Max Verstappen completed 22 efficient laps in Free Practice 1 with a best of 1:38.157 – placing him 12th, one behind Felipe Massa, one in front of Sergio Perez. Franz Tost had told him not to push, take it easy, enjoy yourself (don't crash). He ended up just 0.443 behind temporary team-mate Daniil Kvyat at a circuit he'd never driven, in a car he'd never driven. Max being Max revealed he could have gone quicker. He was awed by the power now under his right foot.

If anything overwhelmed him, it was the amount of engineer radio traffic: 'Just listening through all the messages coming through it was quite a lot. I thought, "Wow that's a lot of information you're giving the driver all the time".'

For someone who'd been used to minimal feedback and set-up changes in Formula 3, now the information was coming thick and fast. 'There are more people around you and people can control everything,' he said, his eyes having been opened wide to the depth of a session debrief. 'You have to discuss a lot, you do that in F3 but now it is more calculated. I think an F1 car is never easy to drive. At least it is not easy for me. Once you go on the limit it is never easy to drive a racing car.'

Helmut was relieved. Franz Tost was impressed. Had Max put the STR9 in the barriers then both of them would have had blame to share. 'Max did not have a problem with the speed which means he was not overloaded by driving,' said Tost. 'Young drivers coming to F1, at the beginning they are passengers, the car is driving them. Not Max, he was driving the car, he could react and he did not spin and he did not crash. The more skilled a driver is the faster he adapts to these challenges... He immediately controlled the car.'

There were two more opportunities for Max to take part in free practice and acclimatize to the massive jump of power between F3 and F1; at Austin for the US Grand Prix and at Interlagos for the Brazilian Grand Prix. Both times he returned the car safely for JEV to continue in Free Practice 2.

In Austin he was tenth fastest and in Brazil he was sixth fastest. Brazil was not without its moment of jeopardy though, a moment captured by the television cameras. As Max guns his Toro Rosso around the downhill Turn 11, the back of the car steps out with a snap of oversteer. He immediately applies opposite lock, the front wheel mounts the kerb as the car drifts to 45 degrees to the direction of travel, and then in an instant it is straight again. Max reduces speed and carries on. Nothing to see here.

The camera switches to the pitwall and a gobsmacked JEV smiles at the screen, mouth agape, while Franz Tost and other engineers exchange nervous smiles. This is a foretaste of things to come.

There was plenty of simulator work to be done, but the last track action of 2014 was the annual Macau Grand Prix, an F3 race round the streets of the former Portuguese enclave in southern China. Max was back with his Van Amersfoort

team for the event and keen to round off the year with a win at a race previously won by the likes of Ayrton Senna, Michael Schumacher and David Coulthard.

In the qualifying race on Saturday Max was second on Lap 4, looking good for a front row start, but crashed the car going for the lead, much to the dismay of Van Amersfoort engineer Rob Niessink. Before the race he'd advised the Verstappens that top three on the grid for Saturday would be good enough, because with slipstreaming on the fast street track, he could easily win from there. Jos said to him, 'What do you mean by top three is good enough? Don't be ridiculous, we need to win.'

Niessink cites this as part of the father and son mentality that only winning is good enough, P2 is the first of the losers. In an interview with the Formula Scout website he recalled the Macau race. 'We were on our way to come home second in the Saturday race where we know we would have absolutely won the main race on Sunday. But for the simple reason that only winning is good enough, Max crashed the car when he was second (meaning he had to start from the back of the grid) and on Sunday he came from the back to P7.

'That's what by nature is in them. It's such an extreme winning mentality that goes beyond anything you normally see. That ridiculous drive is in both of them. They do not accept not being first. Everything needs to move over to achieve that and that goes to a level which you can hardly imagine.'

In a wide-ranging interview with Formule1.nl in 2023 Max confirmed that shared attitude. 'When I was younger I would always say "I'm not like my dad". But the older I get the more I notice how much alike we are: the energy I put into everything, how seriously I take that and the time spent on this. That perpetual drive to reach perfection I definitely inherited from him. And at the end of the day, these are all good and desirable attributes, in my opinion. The world is full of talented people, but there are also a lot of lazy people. It's almost always the case those who work harder make it further. Those who settle for second or third place eventually drop off and those who hate coming second or third, who always keep pushing and never give up, those are the ones who tend to make it.'

In 2015, that natural drive would have to be suppressed. Only one driver had ever won an F1 race in a Toro Rosso – Sebastian Vettel. But ambitious targets had never stopped Team Verstappen.

**TORO
ROSSO**

The biggest physical impact on Max Verstappen's life heading into 2015 came in the form of 6'3" Jake Aliker. As Max had already come to appreciate, the G-forces that an F1 car could generate in high-speed corners, such as Suzuka's 130R, were enormous. The strain of 22 laps, completed in fits and starts, was not enough to exhaust the neck muscles he'd generated for F3 cornering. It would be a whole different proposition completing a race simulation in Barcelona testing.

Aliker was an imposing figure, a former MMA trainer who for the last four years had been working with rugby union squads, first for Harlequins and then for the up-and-coming Championship side Jersey Reds. As head of Strength and Conditioning at the rugby club, he was responsible for making sure his players were protected from injuries by building up their core and neck muscles. When he got the job with Red Bull, he moved to a few blocks away from Max, in Belgium, to supervise the transition from F3 driver to F1 driver. Training would now become a daily chore that kept Max from his simulator. Max's website, Verstappen.com, was keen to find out what Jake was going to put their driver through.

'Before we met, he did a bit of training, a lot of endurance stuff, but there wasn't really any overall structured physical training,' said Aliker. 'And that's what I'm focusing on; over the next few years he needs to get used to organized training.'

Red Bull have a major sports department of specialists looking after their athletes, from racing drivers to mountain bikers to snowboarders. Aliker confirmed that Max was now part of 'the programme'. 'We've got people monitoring his

PREVIOUS PAGE: Max in the 2015 Toro Rosso, the STR10.

LEFT: Max has already got one fan at trackside as he waits to start the 2015 Malaysian Grand Prix with Jake Aliker holding the umbrella.

sleep and nutrition and they are preparing a strategy for him. In the meantime, I oversee his nutrition. I'll keep an eye on his weight, make sure he is not too heavy, especially as he is building up muscle and strength ahead of the new season.'

Then came the key question – is Max a disciplined athlete when it comes to training? It got a textbook response. 'He realizes that being in great physical shape is an asset for his career. So far, he has really got stuck in with the exercises and he picks things up really quickly. It's like you would expect from an F1 driver: you give him info, he processes it very quickly and straight away applies those new skills.'

One of the greatest motivations to train was the need to beat his incoming Toro Rosso team-mate. In all motorsport categories the first person you have to beat is the driver with exactly the same machinery as you – they are your benchmark. At Van Amersfoort Racing it had been no problem, his team-mate had been American driver Gustavo Menezes who he'd often outqualify by over a second, in Macau it had been 2.7 seconds. This wasn't going to happen with Carlos Sainz Junior.

ABOVE LEFT:
Launching the STR10
ahead of winter
testing at Jerez in
January 2015.

ABOVE: Carlos and
Max with their
famous dads
donning more
generous Toro
Rosso overalls.

Like Max, Carlos was the son of a famous motorsport father. Carlos Senior had won the World Rally Championship with Toyota in 1990 and 1992, and finished runner-up four times. Before Spain had Fernando Alonso to worship, they had Carlos Sainz. Carlos Junior was three years older than Max, and at 20, a comparative veteran. He had been part of the Red Bull Junior Programme racing single-seaters since 2010, not a last-minute addition like Max. He had won the 2014 Formula Renault 3.5 series and was viewed by many in the paddock to be in pole position to take the next Toro Rosso seat, not least because the team were sponsored by CEPSA, the Spanish oil and gas company.

When Max was announced in 2014 as the driver who would be lining up alongside Daniil Kvyat, the chance to progress to F1 looked to have been put on hold for 2015. Then Vettel jumped ship, Kvyat was promoted and Carlos was announced at the Abu Dhabi Young Driver Test which follows the end-of-season race at Yas Marina. Given Jean-Eric Vergne's performances over the closing races, some of the Formula 1 media were convinced that the Frenchman would get a reprieve.

YOUNGEST F1 POINTS SCORERS

Thanks to Helmut Marko and the Red Bull driver academy, five of the top ten youngest points scorers are Toro Rosso drivers

MAX VERSTAPPEN
17 years, 180 days
2015 Malaysian Grand Prix
Scuderia Toro Rosso

LANCE STROLL
18 years, 225 days
2017 Canadian Grand Prix
Williams

LANDO NORRIS
19 years, 138 days
2019 Bahrain Grand Prix
McLaren

DANIIL KVYAT
19 years, 324 days
2014 Australian Grand Prix
Scuderia Toro Rosso

SEBASTIAN VETTEL
19 years, 349 days
2007 United States Grand Prix
Scuderia Toro Rosso

JAIME ALGUERSUARI
20 years, 12 days
2010 Malaysian Grand Prix
Scuderia Toro Rosso

JENSON BUTTON
20 years, 67 days
2000 Brazilian Grand Prix
BMW-Williams

RICARDO RODRÍGUEZ
20 years, 123 days
1962 Belgian Grand Prix
Ferrari

SÉBASTIEN BUEMI
20 years, 149 days
2009 Australian Grand Prix
Scuderia Toro Rosso

ESTEBAN OCON
20 years, 190 days
2017 Australian Grand Prix
Force India

YOUNGEST DRIVERS TO SCORE A PODIUM FINISH

Oscar Piastri scored a podium finish in his rookie season, but at 22 he was still too old to get into the top ten.

Max Verstappen
2016 Spanish Grand Prix
Toro Rosso
 18 years 228 days

Lance Stroll
2017 Azerbaijan Grand Prix
Williams
 18 years 239 days

Lando Norris
2020 Austrian Grand Prix
McLaren
 20 years 235 days

Sebastian Vettel
2008 Italian Grand Prix
Toro Rosso
 21 years 73 days

Daniil Kvyat
2015 Hungarian Grand Prix
Toro Rosso
 21 years 91 days

Kevin Magnussen
2014 Australian Grand Prix
McLaren
 21 years 162 days

Charles Leclerc
2019 Bahrain Grand Prix
Ferrari
 21 years 166 days

Fernando Alonso
2003 Malaysian Grand Prix
Renault
 21 years 237 days

Robert Kubica
2006 Italian Grand Prix
BMW-Sauber
 21 years 278 days

Ralf Schumacher
1997 Argentine Grand Prix
Jordan
 21 years 287 days

'This is very interesting,' Sky Sports pitlane reporter Ted Kravitz commented. 'What it means is that Toro Rosso, a team which is usually a midfield runner, is going into the 2015 season with two drivers who between them have done zero grands prix. Two rookies, and that is a big risk – especially when Verstappen is only 17 years old.'

Hindsight is a wonderful thing, but Kravitz was right. With an average age under 19 it was the youngest F1 pairing in history. Taking two rookies into a season, neither of whom had experience of running long stints on the Pirelli tyres, was a gamble. They would have the benefit of pre-season testing in Barcelona in February, but that would be on one circuit, run in wintry conditions they were unlikely to encounter the rest of the year.

The potential problems of rookie team-mates was ably demonstrated by the Haas line-up of Mick Schumacher and Nikita Mazepin in 2021. Strapped-for-cash team boss Guenther Steiner had gone for the sponsorship his two drivers could bring in over their racing potential. In a season when the perennially frustrated Steiner had real problems keeping the duo from colliding with each other, they scored zero points between them and Haas were relegated to 10th and final place in the constructors' table, their worst since joining the grid in 2016.

After early-season testing in Barcelona and Jerez, the Formula 1 juggernaut flew into Melbourne for the season curtain-raiser around Albert Park. Since switching from Adelaide, the Melbourne race was traditionally the first grand prix on the calendar, with a high attrition rate for cars which had yet to iron out gremlins uncovered in testing.

The first FIA press conference of the year on the Thursday before practice was a chance to interview six drivers – and the FIA requested the current world champ Lewis Hamilton, Sebastian Vettel, Daniel Ricciardo, and Max Verstappen got the drop over Carlos Sainz as the representative rookie. Max managed to steer his way round all the predictable questions and smile. They were no problem – he had heard them all before. Lewis suddenly realized he was the oldest driver there and had signed his first McLaren contract in 1997, the year Max was born, and Seb was particularly encouraging. 'I think that despite the fact that Max is still young, I think he has a lot of experience. He's quick, otherwise he wouldn't be here, so I don't think he needs much advice. Take it easy, maybe.'

On Saturday, Max qualified 12th despite setting the fourth fastest time in Q1. He might have made it through to Q3 at his very first attempt but a snap of oversteer at Turn 4 on his fastest lap in Q2 put paid to that. Carlos made it through

to Q3 and claimed eighth on the grid. Advantage Sainz Junior.

The start of the Australian Grand Prix has seen some spectacular accidents over the years with Ralf Schumacher being launched into the air on the run down to the first turn in 2002 (and in 2023 a late-race re-start saw multiple accidents at Turns 1 and 2). As the lights went out, both Max and Carlos heeded Franz Tost's warning to keep their cars in one piece, even if was at the expense of a place.

ABOVE: It was a confident debut in Melbourne, ruined by reliability issues.

The high casualty rate in Melbourne might see both cars in the points. Toro Rosso split the strategy with Carlos starting on softs and Max on the medium tyre.

Motor Sport magazine's Mark Hughes was full of praise for Max's handling of the opening stint: 'Verstappen on his prime tyres kept the soft-tyred Sainz in sight until the latter's pit-stop. Max then stayed out a further eight laps, nailing a hard and consistent pace, driving with great panache – aggressive yet super-precise. He was set to have been fighting Hulkenberg for seventh before the engine broke on his out-lap.'

Having just emerged from the pits on Lap 33, Max radioed back to his engineer in an agitated voice, 'Check the car because it's smoking I think. The engine sounds heavy.' The Renault V6 hybrid engine had indeed expired and Max was left to park his car before the pit entrance. The senior team had run their RB11 car in a camouflage livery in testing but nothing could disguise Christian Horner's frustration with the lack of progress on the Renault engine, and Max's retirement with the 2015 unit meant it was both underpowered *and* potentially unreliable.

Carlos had suffered a 20-second pit-stop when a tyre gun jammed. He also had to drive around an engine mapping problem but managed to bring his car home a lap down in ninth place.

So it was the Spaniard who would be the latest F1 driver to score points on debut. Max was left to reflect on what might have been. He might have been seventh, and at the next grand prix in Malaysia, he was.

ABOVE RIGHT: One race later and Max was able to trade positions with the senior team at the Malaysian Grand Prix.

THE RACE

FORMULA 1
Malaysian Grand Prix
Sepang International Circuit, Malaysia
29 March, 2015

Max joined Toro Rosso at a time when the Australian Grand Prix in Melbourne was the traditional curtain-raiser for the F1 season, but his dream of scoring points on his debut went up in smoke. With his detractors' eyes very much fixed on the 17-year-old, Max qualified in 12th and was heading for a points finish when smoke started emerging from his Renault engine on Lap 34 and he was asked to pull over. So far, so good. No blemishes for Max and it was Carlos who'd tagged his front wing on the back of Kimi Räikkönen's Ferrari.

The second race on the calendar was the Malaysian Grand Prix in Sepang and surely this would present a real problem for the teenager. The heat and humidity of

the Malaysian race was known to test the toughest drivers, with a serious danger of heat fatigue and dehydration, as Jenson Button explained to *Autosport*.

'One time I lost my water bottle and just couldn't get any drink at all. I was so wet (with perspiration) that I started shivering for the last 20 laps of the race, it was pretty scary,' he said. 'Then your vision starts going, after that you dehydrate.'

Former Red Bull racer Mark Webber agrees. 'There's no escape, it's just the heat. Your chest, your head, how hot everything gets. You're just screaming for something a bit cooler from somewhere but there

ABOVE: Carlos and Max try and keep cool on the Sepang grid.

LEFT: In the race Max managed to keep his Toro Rosso ahead of both Red Bulls and finish seventh.

is no place to hide.'

So into the furnace of Sepang stepped young Max Verstappen for his second race in what was Formula 1's most gruelling event. In qualifying, Carlos Sainz made it through to Q2 but could only manage P15, while Max negotiated typical Q2 traffic chaos to put himself into the final part, Q3. And then the heavens opened, forcing all ten runners to fit intermediate tyres. Verstappen then proceeded to demonstrate the level of skill in wet conditions that had so impressed Helmut Marko in his Norisring victories, he put his Toro Rosso STR 10 a remarkable sixth on the grid, just behind the two Red Bull cars of Ricciardo and Kvyat, who were fourth and fifth.

The race was dry, run in searing temperatures and interrupted early on by a safety car after a Marcus Ericsson crash, but Max drove steadily, changing early from medium tyres to hard tyres and managing his brakes throughout, something that the senior team had problems with. 'I really enjoyed that,' he told reporters after the race, looking uncannily fresh. He had finished seventh – the last unlapped driver – and in doing so had become the youngest ever driver to score world championship points. He had also finished in front of his team-mate and both Red Bulls.

'The first few laps were a bit tricky for me as I was struggling a lot on the medium tyres, so we pitted early for the hard ones and that worked perfectly; the car felt great. We had a few good fights with other competitors and it was good fun,' was Max's typical upbeat and understated analysis of the race.

Jacques Villeneuve was at the circuit to watch his dire prediction of teenage disaster proven hopelessly wrong. Max had demonstrated in the harshest conditions that he belonged on the F1 grid. The dog had barked but the caravan had moved on.

Just as Kimi Räikkönen's first races had quietened the critics, so Max's strong race in Malaysia (see Greatest Races page 92) ably demonstrated that he could not only qualify and race well – like a driver of 22 as Helmut Marko had predicted – but he could do so in extreme conditions. But now there was an unexpected threat to Verstappen's F1 future.

Having seen Mercedes run away with the constructors' championship in 2014 with their superior hybrid engine, Christian Horner became increasingly frustrated with his unreliable and slow Renault engine unit. The combination of Red Bull and Renault had been the class of the field, taking the drivers' and constructors' titles in 2010, 2011, 2012 and 2013. But that was fast becoming a distant memory as both Red Bull and the similarly engined Toro Rosso struggled for pace.

Following the Australian Grand Prix Horner hit out at Renault, describing them as 'a bit of a mess', and calling on the FIA, F1's governing body, to consider implementing an equalization mechanism to bring the Mercedes cars within reach. 'The problem is the gap is so big. You end up with three-tier racing and I think that's not healthy for Formula 1,' Horner said, articulating that F1 was losing viewers because of one team's dominance.

Helmut Marko was asked if Red Bull might consider withdrawing from next year's championship if they couldn't make progress on equalization. Helmut, never one to avoid throwing fuel on the fire, responded: 'If we are totally dissatisfied we could contemplate an F1 exit. The danger is there that Mr Mateschitz loses his passion for F1.'

ABOVE LEFT: Max enjoying a taste of the Monaco lifestyle with father Jos at the 2015 Monaco Grand Prix.

ABOVE: Streaking into the Monaco tunnel in the STR10.

Many thought it was a bluff, but it was a bluff that started to creep into the mindset of Jos Verstappen and Raymond Vermeulen. Having shown so much dominance in the Vettel era, neither Mercedes nor Ferrari were keen to give their rivals Red Bull, an engine which, in an Adrian Newey-designed chassis, could beat them. It was important for Max to show exactly what he could do in his first season, just in case the grid suddenly got smaller.

The Blue Riband event of the F1 calendar has always been the Monaco Grand Prix and as the teams convened in the principality for the sixth race of 2014, the more experienced Carlos Sainz was slightly edging Max. He was leading 3–2 in the qualifying battle, though the deficits either way had never been big.

In Spain, the previous race, Toro Rosso had embarrassed the senior team in qualifying with Carlos fifth and Max sixth ahead of both Red Bulls. Another vindication of Helmut Marko's faith in his rookies. Max came home 11th, Carlos ninth. By the time they got to Monaco, Carlos had three points finishes to his name, Max had the solitary seventh place from Malaysia. But the good news for both Red Bull teams was that success at Monaco does not require the most powerful engine. This would be the race where a nimble Adrian Newey-designed chassis could score points.

Max started the weekend in impressive style. On his first visit to the principality he had followed the old Verstappen maxim – go out hard and fast – and set the second fastest time in the very first practice session. In qualifying on Saturday he looked to have got the better of Carlos too, setting the sixth fastest time in Q2, faster than Daniel Ricciardo and almost half a second quicker than Sainz. All four Red Bull organization cars were through to Q3, but it was Max who failed to improve in the final segment and he ended up tenth, behind Maldonado's Lotus in ninth and Carlos in eighth.

However, Sainz had made a serious rookie error, an error amplified by the fact that overtaking in Monaco is so difficult. In the tight and busy Monaco pitlane he had missed a random weighbridge request in Q1 – the penalty for which was exclusion from the qualifying results. He would have to start his grand prix from the pitlane and join the rest of the pack as they were speeding up the hill through Beau Rivage.

In the race, Max kept it out of trouble on the opening lap, but found himself stuck behind Maldonado's Lotus. The Venezuelan was suffering from a hydraulic leak and falling back from the car in front with Verstappen right on his gearbox.

Overtaking 'in anger' at the end of the start/finish straight into the St Dévote corner is rarely possible, usually only seen when cars are lapping a backmarker.

Similar to his overtaking move on Felipe Nasr at Spa later in the year, Max had yet to realize this was a fact of F1 life. Maldonado saw him coming up the inside and the pair passed through the tight first corner just millimetres apart. Max took the place in the drag race up to Massenet with the most audacious pass of the race.

Then disaster. Hoping to undercut the Force India of Sergio Perez with an earlier pit-stop, the Toro Rosso pitcrew experienced problems with the wheel nut on his right rear wheel, which had to be taken off and refitted, an agonizing delay of 20 stationary seconds. Max rejoined behind Valtteri Bottas and, with little prospect of getting past the Finn's Williams unassisted, waited for Vettel to lap them both, then snuck past on the inside into Portier as the Ferrari swept through, elevating him to 11th place. He then set off in pursuit of Romain Grosjean in the second Lotus.

Max's tyres were in far better condition than Grosjean's, but there are few traction races at Monaco where it can make the difference. He tried to sneak

ABOVE: Marshals help Max from the car after he crashed into the barriers at St Dévote.

ABOVE RIGHT: Max had raced at Silverstone before, but his F1 debut ended in the gravel.

past down to the Grand Hotel hairpin when a Ferrari came up to lap them and the blue flags were waved, but the Frenchman was wise to the move. Perhaps he could try the same route that was successful with Pastor Maldonado?

On Lap 64 Max was shaping up for a dive down the inside at St Dévote when Grosjean braked and the Toro Rosso thumped into the rear of the Lotus, sending Max straight for the barriers and a 30G impact.

Max had misjudged it as Grosjean was having to brake earlier on old, worn tyres. 'The data shows I actually braked five metres later than on the lap before. He was just way, way too late with his move,' Grosjean said after the race, indignant that the rookie had ruined his chance of points. He labelled Max 'dangerous'. From a driver with a rich pedigree of rash, early race collisions, a man once described by Mark Webber as 'that first-lap nutcase', this was rich.

Max was slow to get out of the car wedged underneath the TecPro barrier, but physically fine, convinced that the accident had been caused by Grosjean's swiftness on the brakes.

The stewards thought otherwise and handed Max a five-place grid drop for the next race in Canada. It was Max's first big mistake in Formula 1, but he shook it off. 'Without a doubt it was my biggest crash,' he told his website, 'you just see the barrier come towards you and you're thinking "I really have to brace myself". You know you're about to crash. But that crash is behind me now.' Subsequently he thought that the crash might have improved him. 'For me it gave me more confidence. You're always a bit scared to crash or even touch a wall, but now I had a big crash and it all gets a bit more relaxed.'

And looking on the bright side, Verstappen's crash and his delaying of Grosjean had handed tenth place to Carlos.

The next race on the calendar where handling and tyre management would be far more important than sheer power was the Hungaroring in August. The tarmac surface at Budapest, combined with the short in-lap that cuts out the final

turn, lends itself to two- and three-pit-stop races. Many people describe the layout as more like a kart track than a grand prix circuit so Max should have been in his element. Max was not so sure and described it with typical Verstappen bluntness: 'I've raced at the Hungaroring in Formula 3, and it's a bit of a Mickey Mouse track.'

Red Bull and Toro Rosso had suffered three miserable retirements from the British Grand Prix, but at Budapest, in a chaotic race of collisions, safety cars and strategy calls, Daniil Kvyat came home second, Daniel Ricciardo finished alongside him on the podium in third, with Max scoring his highest finish to date, in fourth place. Naturally, in this season of firsts, it was the first time a 17-year-old had finished fourth in a grand prix.

'Unbelievable, P4 – what a great result, I have no words,' Max told reporters after the race. His age, as ever, was the focus of interest to the wider press who revelled in the

knowledge that his day job was driving an F1 car at speeds of up to 200mph but if he wanted to go out in a road car in Belgium, he'd have to take his mum. 'I'm doing my lessons in the summer break and then will take my driving test around my birthday in September, when I'm 18,' he revealed, keen to finally ruin a good story. 'With the F1 schedule it has been difficult to fit everything in so I've had to wait for the break. You need a minimum six or seven hours' driving under the laws in Belgium, where I live – and I hope that's all I need.'

Before he could take that test there was his home grand prix at Spa-Francorchamps. That's the home grand prix based on his birthplace, his mother's nationality, where he had gone to school, lived all his life and lived now. His Dutch father had registered him on a Dutch racing licence, thus ensuring in the future he would have two home grands prix, with the Austrian Grand Prix also appended by the Oranje Army and the Monaco Grand Prix a possibility too, in years to come.

Spa was a circuit where he had scored three important wins in his European Formula 3 season and where he had a tremendous amount of confidence. So in Q1 on Saturday it was with a sinking feeling that he realized his engine was down on power. He struggled into Q2 in P15 but that was his session done. He didn't emerge for the next segment and a change of engine unit ensured a further 10-place grid drop. The fact that the replacement engine was still a Renault meant that he would be struggling to make up places on the long Spa straights and high-speed curves – the only way he could compete was to strip back the rear

ABOVE LEFT: Toro Rosso mechanics celebrate as Max finishes fourth at the Hungaroring, the team's best finish of the year and something he would repeat in Austin.

LEFT: Posing with a fan holding the Limburgian flag at the 2015 Belgian GP. The lion motif would soon appear on Max's helmet.

RIGHT: Max turns in to Les Combes at the top of the Kemmel Straight in Spa, 2015.

wing elements to minimum downforce and try and hold on in the slower, middle sector of the circuit.

Max was slow off the line and passed by others who had slipped behind him on the grid after their engine penalties, but he carefully picked his way through the pack at La Source hairpin and was soon past Räikkönen, Button and Alonso on the inside of Turn 15, Blanchimont. Three world champions in a row. Later in the race he went side by side with Felipe Nasr's Sauber on the outside of Blanchimont at speeds of close to 190mph.

The two cars flashed through side by side with Max's STR 10 looking very stable as the car ran out wide over the kerbing. It brought a sharp intake of breath from David Croft and Martin Brundle in the Sky TV commentary box.

'They know no fear, do they?' Brundle chuckled admiringly, not quite sure what he had witnessed, '200mph corner, round the outside on the kerb and keep your foot pinned, don't think of lifting.'

Max knew he could do it, because he'd done it in the sim.

Verstappen hadn't actually overtaken Nasr because he was off the road and would have been made to give the place back, and Felipe slowed to let Max through at the Bus Stop chicane that followed as he needed to get across into the pitlane, but Max had no idea he was pitting. It had been a bravura performance from Verstappen nevertheless. It also won him the FIA 'Action of the Year' award at season's end. He finished the race in eighth, quite a result for an underpowered car that had started near the back of the grid.

After the race Max returned to Belgium for an appointment with a driving test examiner. It would have been a front page story in *De Telegraaf* if he had failed, but he got close. 'Once I didn't give way,' Max told his website, 'but they were like miles behind so I didn't see it necessary to stop. So I just continued, but clearly the examiner thought differently.' He passed.

With that hurdle overcome, the next big step was an immediate move to an apartment in Monaco. He wouldn't be alone. Jake Aliker, his trainer, would be coming with him, but after more than 13 years he would be stepping away from day-to-day fatherly supervision.

Helmut Marko put it delicately. 'When Jos recognized that his "baby" was in good hands he saw that his role is, not over, but is less important. So in the beginning there were some times he thought he should be involved more, but he learned quickly. Red Bull made a deal that he is not coming to all grands prix and now he's coming less and less.'

MAX VS THE WORLD

Max Verstappen vs Italy

The tifosi might give Max a hard time, but when it comes to winning grands prix, it's the Red Bull driver way out in front.

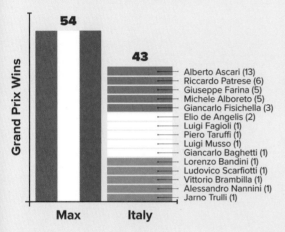

54 Max
43 Italy

- Alberto Ascari (13)
- Riccardo Patrese (6)
- Giuseppe Farina (5)
- Michele Alboreto (5)
- Giancarlo Fisichella (3)
- Elio de Angelis (2)
- Luigi Fagioli (1)
- Piero Taruffi (1)
- Luigi Musso (1)
- Giancarlo Baghetti (1)
- Lorenzo Bandini (1)
- Ludovico Scarfiotti (1)
- Vittorio Brambilla (1)
- Alessandro Nannini (1)
- Jarno Trulli (1)

Max Verstappen vs Australia

Daniel Ricciardo and Oscar Piastri are still contenders on the F1 grid, but it's the Dutchman who's the master.

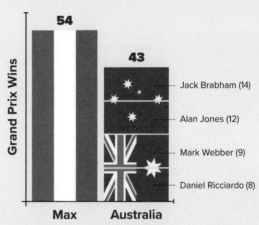

54 Max
43 Australia

- Jack Brabham (14)
- Alan Jones (12)
- Mark Webber (9)
- Daniel Ricciardo (8)

Max Verstappen vs Finland

Finland has produced some extraordinary drivers in the past, but Max is fast approaching the total of the ice men.

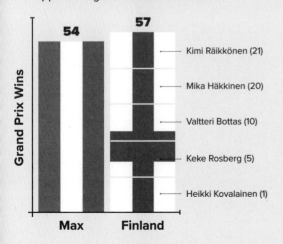

54 Max
57 Finland

- Kimi Räikkönen (21)
- Mika Häkkinen (20)
- Valtteri Bottas (10)
- Keke Rosberg (5)
- Heikki Kovalainen (1)

Max Verstappen vs Austria

Like Finland, Austria punches above its weight in grand prix victories, but Max is pulling clear.

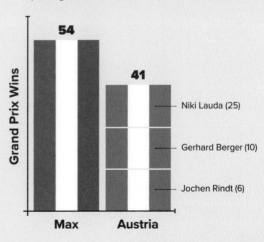

54 Max
41 Austria

- Niki Lauda (25)
- Gerhard Berger (10)
- Jochen Rindt (6)

That didn't mean to say that Jos was excluded from his career the way Lewis Hamilton had fallen out with his father Anthony, who had been his manager and was replaced by a management team. Jos and Raymond were still involved in every decision made, but now, an 18-year-old Max had the ultimate power to say 'no'.

And say 'no' was exactly what he did at the Singapore Grand Prix. Towards the end of the race, running line astern at the Marina Bay track, the two Toro Rossos were in eighth and ninth places, both shod with supersoft tyres. Max was leading Carlos but could find no way past the Force India of Sergio Perez ahead of them. Carlos, whose tyres were a lap fresher, asked the team if they could move Max aside to play the team game... 'and let the guy on a newer tyre, that was me, try, at least to have one shot,' said Sainz after the race. 'If I can't get past Perez, we swap back. I just wanted one shot, [but] he never gave it to me. It's not an issue for me, but sometimes you have to think about the team and not just yourself.'

Verstappen was twice asked to let Sainz go by and refused. Max had endured a tough grand prix, he'd been wheeled off the grid, gone a lap down and heroically clawed his way back into the points after a safety car period. He didn't think Carlos was even close enough to challenge him with his new tyres, let alone Perez who was going away on the straights.

Team boss Franz Tost said after the race that Max had made the right call. 'I said over team radio if Carlos is not close then it makes no sense to swap

ABOVE: The 2015 USGP was plagued by bad weather, but Max produced another strong showing and finished fourth.

LEFT: Flashpoint in Singapore: Max is trailed by Carlos, but refuses to move over.

RIGHT: Despite the friction caused by the Singapore row, Max and Carlos enjoyed a good relationship in 2015.

positions because he would never get Perez as he is too far behind – between three and five tenths behind. Sainz should have shown at first he was capable of overtaking Max before then trying to catch Perez.'

The question that lay unanswered was: If Franz Tost thought that, why did the team give the instruction to move over in the first place? Some in the paddock saw it as a case of finding a suitable excuse after the fact, a case of papering over the cracks. What it showed, they argued, was the balance of power – that Verstappen was the driver they had to appease, not Sainz, who simmered.

Certainly the late-season results backed up the view that Max was the growing force. After a fairly even start with Carlos, he was beginning to accelerate away. For Helmut Marko it was a reassuring success curve for a man in only his second season of single-seaters. From the fourth place in Hungary to the end of the season he scored points finishes in eight of the final ten races, Carlos scoring points only three times.

At the end of the season Max had scored 49 points with four retirements, Carlos had scored 11 points with seven retirements. Max's results included another starring fourth place, this time at the US Grand prix in Austin. The weather had been so bad on Saturday that qualifying had to be moved to the Sunday and even that had to be abandoned after heavy rain in Q2, with all positions taken from the end of the second period.

The race was started on a drying track with cars on intermediates. Max made his way forward from tenth on the grid and had a testy, early-race battle with Kimi Räikkönen's Ferrari, the two cars making contact at one point. The normally taciturn 'Ice Man' was surprised that Max had been allowed to get away with late braking moves and pushing him off the track and (for Kimi) was quite long-winded in his call for FIA clarification after the race.

'I just wanted to ask if it's okay when you are next to another car, at some point on the exit of the corner are you allowed to always push the other car up on the kerbs,' Räikkönen told *Autosport*. 'As long as everybody has the same rules that's okay. There are so many rules in F1 these days: you should not move under braking, you should leave a car's space when the other guy is next to you... I don't complain he [Verstappen] is doing anything wrong, as long as it's fine the next time someone else does it in the same way.'

ABOVE: Max in front of a less-than-happy Kimi Räikkönen in Austin.

This wasn't the last time the duo would be the intense focus of race cameras in a grand prix, and the next time, yet again, Max would come out on top.

RED BULL

The 2016 season was the start of what would become a familiar trend in Max's career. His ability to lose team-mates. Before Formula 1 reconvened for the opening race in Melbourne, Max knew that he was going to lose one at the end of the year. He had decisively won the unofficial battle of the rookies with Carlos Sainz in 2015 and other teams were keen to find out his future availability.

PREVIOUS PAGE:
Max exits Mirabeau
at Monaco in 2016.

LEFT: The Red Bull
Class of 2016 at a
pre-season event in
Kitzbühel, Austria,
with Canadian ski
racer Erik Guay
taking the selfie.
Max, Daniel, Daniil,
Carlos and MotoGP
rider Marc Marquez.

BELOW: The
team-mates pose in
the Bahrain garage
before Round 2.

It was not as though Team Verstappen owed a huge debt to the Red Bull Junior Programme. Carlos Sainz, Alex Albon, Daniel Ricciardo – they had all been funded much earlier in their careers. Red Bull had funded Max with less than half of the European Formula 3 season to go. Helmut Marko had the budget, and a race seat, and was keen to trump his old Austrian rival Niki Lauda at Mercedes who had been showing serious interest. Now it was Ferrari and McLaren who were making enquiries about Max's availability at the end of his contract with Toro Rosso/Red Bull.

Ferrari knew that Kimi Räikkönen's time at the Scuderia was playing out and, similarly, McLaren had two quite senior drivers in Jenson Button and Fernando Alonso who were losing patience in the lack of progress with their Honda engine. To ward off any potential suitor, the Verstappens got an assurance that come the start of the 2017 season, Max would be sitting in a Red Bull next to Daniel Ricciardo. The fuse had been lit for Daniil Kvyat.

For now, all was set for another learning season in F1. Christian Horner in the Red Bull team would continue to push Renault to develop the engine shared by all four cars, but there had been some progress since his post-Australian Grand Prix rant of 2015. Early-season results bore this out with Daniel Ricciardo finishing fourth in the

first three races, as Andrew Davies succinctly noted in his Planet F1.com column: 'Daniel is destined to become the new Nick Heidfeld – forever finishing fourth'.

Max scored three points finishes in the first three races for Toro Rosso, keeping his nose in front of Carlos in each. He made it into Q3 for the Russian Grand Prix at Sochi while Sainz was eliminated in Q2, but in the race, a power unit failure ended any hopes of four points finishes in a row.

Meanwhile, in the senior team, Daniil Kvyat was causing havoc with Scuderia Ferrari. At the third race of the year, the Chinese Grand Prix in Shanghai, a 'torpedo' move from Daniil at the start of the race had squeezed Sebastian Vettel into team-mate Kimi Räikkönen, half-spinning the Finn's Ferrari and removing its front wing as it struck the Red Bull. Vettel survived and went on to finish the race in P2, but he was not impressed. 'Okay, I made contact,' he reported on the first lap. 'I had no chance to avoid, I had the Red Bull coming up the inside like a madman and I hit Kimi.'

Kvyat showed the serious potential of the new RB11 by scoring a podium in P3. Christian Horner's post-race comments gave little indication to what was going to happen next. 'It's been a great day for the team, especially after that unfortunate start. For Daniel to take the lead and then get that puncture was desperately unlucky... Dany took up the baton and drove a fantastic race, racing with Sebastian for a large part of the race to achieve his second podium. A third and fourth place finish, lots of constructors points so yes, a great day for the team.'

In Sochi, the nature of the Kvyat/Vettel spat worsened considerably and was the catalyst for the kind of mid-season team swap that Red Bull would repeat in the Max Verstappen era.

LEFT: Max in action at the Sakhir circuit, Bahrain. He finished a promising sixth.

BELOW: He took eighth place in his penultimate drive for Toro Rosso at Shanghai.

BELOW RIGHT: A promotional photo from the Chinese GP. Joker Max is about to swap his overalls for some shiny ones.

Racing at his home grand prix in front of Russian president Vladimir Putin, Daniil Kvyat had a demolition derby of an opening lap. After locking up and nerfing the Ferrari of Sebastian Vettel into Daniel Ricciardo at Turn 2, Kvyat well and truly torpedoed into a slowing Vettel in the long, fast right-hander at Turn 3, spinning him into the barrier.

Vettel, who saw his chance of challenging Nico Rosberg for the 2016 championship disappear in three corners, was explosively angry, turning team radio blue.

'Oh, for ****'s sake!' he screamed. 'Somebody hit me in the ****ing rear! Turn 2! And then somebody hit me in the ****ing rear again in Turn 3. Honestly! What the **** are we doing here?' It certainly got the unofficial FIA award for 'Team Radio Moment of the Year'.

That ire didn't disappear when he found out it was the same person, Daniil Kvyat. Helmut Marko was embarrassed that one of his drivers had managed a double hit on one of his former protégés. At the Spanish Grand Prix in 2015 he had been scathing when the two 'exceptional' Toro Rosso drivers had outqualified Kvyat. 'Our established guys need to look out,' Helmut told *Kleine Zeitung.* 'Paradoxically, the more inexperienced ones did the better job.'

Kvyat had improved his performances in the latter half of 2015 and even finished ahead of Ricciardo in the drivers' championship. It was enough for Christian Horner to keep the same line-up for 2016. 'Both the drivers are on long-term contracts, but it's a successful partnership and it's working well.'

Daniil was watching the HBO series *Game of Thrones,* the fantasy drama filled with back-stabbing twists, when he got the call from Helmut Marko that he was moving back to Toro Rosso. 'There was no real explanation to be honest. If the bosses want something to happen they just make it happen,' Kvyat revealed at the following race. 'The decision was a bit of a shock. I was standing on the podium (in China) three weeks ago,' the 22-year-old said. 'But it is what it is. I have always given my answers on the track and I think nothing will change.'

Christian Horner was keen to explain that it wasn't simply one errant race that had sparked the move. 'We are privy to a lot of information going back to the start of testing and Daniil has been struggling for form against his team-mate,' said the Red Bull team principal. 'The race in Russia was a catalyst but a lot more consideration went into it than one Sunday afternoon.'

He was also keen to emphasize the opportunity it presented with Max

alongside the talented and hugely likeable Daniel Ricciardo. 'Make no mistake, Max is one of the hottest properties in Formula 1. People said it was too early for Max when he got his debut at 17 but he is now one of the most exciting things in the sport.' Horner also revealed that with the 'sharks' circling, Red Bull had used the event to sign a fresh deal with Verstappen tying him to the team until 2020.

Sky Sport's Martin Brundle was full of praise for the team's canny switch: 'They know Ferrari will want him, they know Mercedes will want him, it's a bit of a master stroke by Red Bull.' Max first learned about the proposal when Jos rang him. 'I got a call from my dad first, at home in Monaco,' he explained in a Red Bull podcast, 'and he said maybe there's a chance you're driving for Red Bull the next race. And I said, "You're crazy, what are you talking about, I'm a Toro Rosso driver." I didn't believe him and he hung up.

'Then Helmut rang up on the Tuesday and he said, "You have to come to Graz (where he owns two hotels)." So we went for lunch and an hour went by and nothing was mentioned. And then he said, "Oh, by the way, you're driving for Red Bull next race, so get ready".'

There would be no time to step into the car beforehand but at least he knew his way round the Circuit de Catalunya. The FIA then made things excruciatingly awkward for Red Bull and Toro Rosso by requesting both Daniil and Max turn up for the Thursday press conference, and sat them side by side on the front row. James Allen was in charge of proceedings, but put the key question delicately.

James Allen: 'Max Verstappen, obviously you're replacing Daniil at Red Bull, how do you rate the opportunity and the risks involved in this move so early in your career?'

THE RACE

FORMULA 1
Spanish Grand Prix
Circuit de Catalunya, Barcelona, Spain
15 May, 2016

Elevated to the senior team at the expense of Daniil Kvyat, there were many who thought Max would be brought quickly down to earth by his likeable but vastly more experienced new team-mate Daniel Ricciardo. Up until now a fellow rookie had been his benchmark, now he was up against a race-winning driver in his sixth season of Formula 1.

It didn't seem to faze Max in the slightest. Christian Horner was astonished at the speed at which Verstappen adapted. 'He came into the senior team without having tested the car even in the sim. There were few people faster over a single lap than Daniel Ricciardo at that time yet Max walked in, went faster in practice, faster in Q1 and Q2 and only lost out in Q3 because the track grip was ramping up and he was nervous about changing the wing level so picked up a bit of understeer.'

The juggernaut success of the Silver Arrows team in 2016 meant that Ferrari and Red Bull were squabbling for the remaining podium place in Barcelona. Having qualified P3 and P4, Max a respectable 0.4 seconds behind Ricciardo, his major obstacles were getting off the line with a new clutch and to negotiate the first couple of turns without incident. Easier said than done at Circuit de Catalunya.

It was a clean start from the Red Bull duo slotting in behind the Mercedes pair off the line. Polesitter Hamilton had lost the lead to Rosberg on the run down to Turn 1 but as they exited Turn 3, Nico found himself in 'formation lap engine mode' which he'd selected accidentally. Up until that point it had been overridden by 'launch engine mode'. When that dropped out he suddenly lost momentum. Hamilton seized his chance and went for the inside – Rosberg pushed him off the track, and both Mercedes were out on the spot.

Suddenly Red Bull were P1 and P2. Now, there was a very good reason to split the strategy and ensure a Red Bull win, but they needed to out-strategize Ferrari. Ferrari put Sebastian Vettel onto a three-stopper, Kimi Räikkönen remained on a two-stopper. Red Bull would do the same with Daniel and Max, the effective No.1s versus the No.2s.

RIGHT: Max takes a look in his mirrors to see how close Kimi Räikkönen has got, but his front tyres still look in good shape.

When Ricciardo pitted on Lap 11, Max became the first Dutchman ever to lead a grand prix. He also led from Laps 28 to 33 until his own second stop, but from Lap 44 he was in front of the race, with Kimi Räikkönen breathing down his gearbox, waiting for his moment when Max would make a mistake.

He didn't, he won. So tight had been the strategy calls that Daniel Ricciardo couldn't even get on the podium and had to settle for P4 behind Vettel.

'We knew that the two-stop was going to be under a lot of pressure at the end of the race in terms of tyre degradation,' said Horner, 'but Max has been able to look after his tyres incredibly well to make sure that he had just enough left to fend off Kimi over the last five or six laps; just incredible.'

'In the last eight laps Kimi was right with me. It was like driving on ice,' Max reported (something, no doubt, Jos will have made him do in his karting days). 'But I

know it's difficult to overtake here so I just managed the pressure and the tyres – made sure I did no front locking, didn't slide in the last sector, making sure I got a good exit out the chicane.

'I started cramping a bit five laps from the end because of the excitement and the focus. There was a lot of pressure.'

Jos, who is always more nervous than his son before a race, was watching from the driver room and going through the same agonies he would experience five years later, but the emotion after the race was incredible. Journalists who'd known him from his own F1 career, such as David Tremayne and Mark Hughes, were coming up and hugging him.

Max had broken a barrel-load of 'youngest' F1 records in one go. He'd also clinched quite a few 'first Dutch driver to...' records into the bargain. Unlike future Toro Rosso graduates, he would not be reversing back into the junior team.

ABOVE: Max came under the experienced eye of Gianpiero Lambiase (beyond) for the first time in Barcelona.

ABOVE RIGHT: Jake Aliker was still on umbrella duties and would continue training Max until 2019. David Coulthard grabs a word on the grid.

RIGHT: First race, first win – substitutions don't get much better.

Max answered like the professional he had become.

Max: 'To be honest, I'm very happy with the opportunity they've given me. I'm racing for a top team now. That was always the plan. I think it was a bigger risk to be so young in Formula 1, but I've handled it pretty well. It will come race by race and I'm definitely going to enjoy it.'

AGE WHEN WINNING FIRST GRAND PRIX

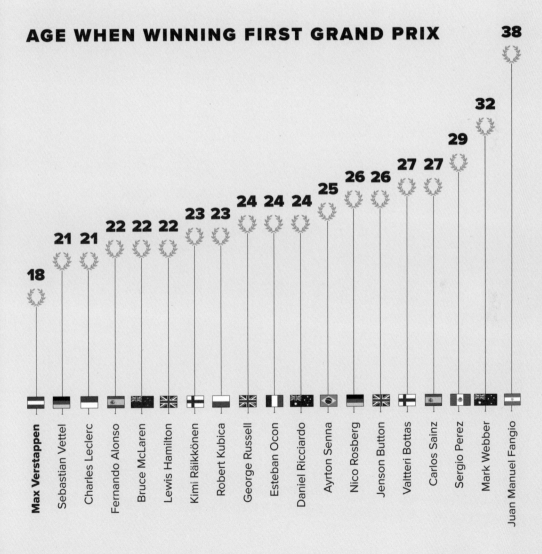

18	21	21	22	22	22	23	23	24	24	24	25	26	26	27	27	29	32	38
Max Verstappen	Sebastian Vettel	Charles Leclerc	Fernando Alonso	Bruce McLaren	Lewis Hamilton	Kimi Räikkönen	Robert Kubica	George Russell	Esteban Ocon	Daniel Ricciardo	Ayrton Senna	Nico Rosberg	Jenson Button	Valtteri Bottas	Carlos Sainz	Sergio Perez	Mark Webber	Juan Manuel Fangio

That may have sounded over-confident, but by late Sunday afternoon Max had justified all the belief placed in him by Marko and Horner by clinching his first race win – and rewriting the record book in the process. (Greatest Races page 114.)

Former Red Bull driver David Coulthard was suitably impressed. 'The circumstances of making a debut and winning the grand prix were just fairytale stuff. What we all now know is that it was just another day in the Max race performance collection. The fact that he didn't know the car, didn't know the team, he seized the opportunity and that's what the great drivers do. They take an opportunity when it comes to them and they deliver.'

Max came back down to earth with a bump at the following race in Monaco. Gunning his Red Bull through the Swimming Pool complex in Q1, he turned into the right-hand exit just a fraction too early. His front-right wheel clattered the barrier, instantly deranging the steering and sending him straight on. The Red Bull was launched over the kerbing and impacted the barrier on exit, shattering the front wing. Qualifying is everything in Monaco and while his new team-mate was putting his Red Bull on pole, Max would be starting from the pitlane, behind everyone bar Nasr. Hero to sub-Zero.

One thing that has characterized the Verstappen career is that he very rarely makes the same mistake twice. However in 2018 he reproduced the exact same accident at the Swimming Pool exit in FP3, requiring his mechanics to embark on a frantic rebuild before qualifying, a few hours later.

In the 2016 race, which started behind the safety car on wet tyres, Max had made his way through to tenth place – remarkable given the limited places to

ABOVE: Max gets squeezed onto the Spa kerbing at La Source hairpin as Vettel cuts across his team-mate.

LEFT: Two images from Max's crunch with the barrier at the Monaco Swimming Pool exit. It wouldn't be the last time his Red Bull would end up there.

overtake – and a dry line was beginning to emerge. Then, following another car too closely up the hill towards Massenet, he lost downforce, skidded wide and ran his car along the barriers. Helmut Marko looked on from his seat in the pit garage without betraying a hint of emotion as Max clambered out of the stricken car. As Jos had predicted, Max was going to have to do a lot of his learning in public.

Following his famous win in Spain, the home interest was growing rapidly, and with no Dutch Grand Prix yet on the calendar, by the time of the Belgian Grand Prix a sell-out crowd was guaranteed. Despite the track being a favourite of F1 drivers and having a racing pedigree that stretches back to the 1930s, Spa has always been dogged financially. Max's success looked to be its saviour.

In 2016 the fans were out in force to watch him duke it out with Kimi Räikkönen's Ferrari up the Kemmel Straight in an epic battle that had the Finn in an irate and unusually talkative mood after the race. At the start, the two Ferraris and Max had come together in a typical opening-lap clash at La Source hairpin, when every car aims for the apex. Max was on the inside, Kimi was in the middle and Vettel moved across on them both – pushing Kimi into Max and Max onto the kerbing, damaging his car. As the race settled down, Kimi tried to get past the now-impaired Red Bull, but Max was employing every trick in the Formula 3 playbook to keep him behind, moving in the braking zones, jinking across on the Kemmel Straight to break the tow (as he'd had to do so many times with Ocon on his fabulous weekend of three F3 wins), washing out wide when Kimi tried to pass round the outside into Les Combes. It was the must-see onboard video of the race, but with a highly compromised car Max could only trail home 11th.

In the media pen afterwards, Kimi was going beyond single sentences. 'Maybe he needs an accident before things become clearer to everybody, but hopefully not, because it can be a bit bad for somebody. And obviously nobody

BELOW: An increasingly irritated Kimi Räikkönen pursues Max during the Belgian GP.

wants to see anybody get hurt. Like I said, I'm fine with racing and fighting hard, but something like that should not be correct, in my view.'

Max was unrepentant, pointing out that he was forced to defend hard because his car had been damaged at the start by the Ferrari. When asked by TV crews if he needed to tone down his driving, Verstappen said: 'To be honest, it's a big lie. I'm just defending my position and if somebody doesn't like it it's his own problem.'

Mercedes boss Toto Wolff was on his side. 'He is refreshing for me. He is a young boy I like a lot. He comes in here with no fear, no respect, puts the elbows out. It reminds me of the great ones – it reminds me of Lewis, of Ayrton Senna. You can see that some guys are starting to think twice about how to overtake him. Until now, all that has proven he is on the right track.'

Though Toto did add a cautionary note: 'I just fear it might end up in the wall heavily one day. It is refreshing but dangerous.' It was a view taken by FIA Race Director Charlie Whiting, who was on hand to advise but not instruct the race stewards at Spa. Before the next race in Monza he took Max aside for a conversation. Whiting was not the typical FIA bureaucrat, but a former Brabham team engineer who'd been chief mechanic on Nelson Piquet's car in the 1980s, moving to work for the FIA when the Brabham team folded. He was widely respected in the pitlane as the unflappable voice of reason.

Whiting told Verstappen that he could have been shown a black-and-white flag for unsportsmanlike behaviour at Spa, and 'could be shown' it in the future.

'The main thrust of what I said to Max is that whilst we like the competitive type of driving he's providing us with, he needs to be careful not to go over the top,' Whiting told Autosport. 'Sometimes he is just a little bit too aggressive, shall we say. He just needs to be careful he doesn't get a bad name for himself because if, heaven forbid, there was an accident caused by what is judged to have been Max's over-exuberant driving then all these things will come back to haunt him.

'He fully accepted it. We had a very amicable chat, and he got the point.'

Though the increasingly acrimonious intra-Mercedes battle between Rosberg and Hamilton was the main feature of 2016, Max Verstappen's overtaking duels were fast becoming the second most compelling reason to watch a grand prix.

In Malaysia, the Red Bull duo locked out the second row of the grid behind both Mercedes. At the start Sebastian Vettel collided with Rosberg, spinning him to the back of the field, promoting the Red Bulls to P2 and P3. The team knew that if they were going to beat Mercedes for another headline-grabbing win they would have to adapt their strategy, and when Daniel radioed back that he could make his tyres last until the end, it effectively put him on a one-stopper and Max on a two. It was a reversal of the Barcelona race, except this time, Daniel was trying to keep his team-mate behind him, not a Ferrari.

Told they were allowed to race, Max used tyre life to harass Ricciardo and Christian Horner held his breath as they raced side by side through Turns 4 to 7. The 'Honey Badger' proved that he was good at both overtaking and defending, keeping Max, on fresher tyres, behind him. When Lewis Hamilton's engine failed moments later they were effectively leading the race and going for the win.

A virtual safety car, called to remove Hamilton's parked Mercedes, allowed Horner the breathing space of bringing both cars in for new tyres, while keeping position. It was then a sprint to the line, with Max closing, closing, closing to 1.1 seconds – about to jump into the DRS zone, when he locked his brakes badly into Turn 15, and that was game over.

After the race Christian Horner was asked if he'd been tempted to impose team orders as he'd done with Vettel and Webber in the past. 'No, different drivers, different characters,' said Horner. 'I trusted that they would race fairly and with respect – and they did.'

It had been Red Bull's first 1–2 finish since 2013. Max and Daniel had enjoyed themselves – Daniel performing his champagne-from-boot drinking party piece on the podium, obliging Max and third-place Rosberg to follow suit. The 'irresponsible' driver of Spa had raced impeccably. 'I had to back out of it at (Turn) 7,' Verstappen admitted, 'because basically I would have been risking us both not finishing.'

'You're in the heat of battle, you're seeing red but at the same time you've got to smile,' grinned Ricciardo, who dedicated the race win to Jules Bianchi. Racing purists had loved it. 'Seeing them race at such close quarters, wheel to wheel through fourth-, fifth- and sixth-gear corners, total trust in each other, was the raw

BELOW LEFT: Neither set of front tyres looks good as Max tries to find a way past Daniel in Malaysia.

BELOW: Daniel performs his party piece, the 'shoey,' after winning in Sepang. Max plays the dutiful team-mate and joins in. Chandon don't recommend that their champagne is served this way.

essence of racing,' wrote an impressed Mark Hughes in *Motor Sport*.

After the race, Sebastian Vettel was handed a three-place grid penalty for causing a collision at the start. 'I was assaulted by a four-time world champion, out of control,' Rosberg said. Ironically it was Sebastian who had been telling Max to take it easy after the Belgian Grand Prix.

It wasn't the last time that Max would provide compelling viewing in the 2016 season. At the penultimate race of the season Verstappen showcased his supreme talent in the wet. All those years of Jos standing on the corners of karting tracks in the pouring rain, showing Max the line he should be taking, came good at Interlagos in the Brazilian Grand Prix (see Greatest Races, page 128).

In changing intensities of rain the race was interrupted by five safety cars and two red flags. Each intervention demanded a strategy call, and though Max had at times run in second place, the team got the penultimate call wrong, sending him out on intermediates.

Finally switching to the full wet tyre with 15 laps to go, he found himself down in 14th place. Verstappen carried spellbound onboard viewers with him (check it out on YouTube) on his charge though to third place in a performance some likened to Senna at Donington in 1993, when the great Brazilian had carved through the field on the opening lap as though driving in a different formula. Senna, like Max, was a karting genius. Apart from his podium trophy and a

LEFT: The 2016 Brazilian Grand Prix was run in between torrential rain showers and Max was in his element.

RIGHT: An end-of-season Red Bull promotion before the Abu Dhabi Grand Prix. Max and Daniel were the perfect foils for some of Red Bull's most imaginative marketing events.

driver-of-the-day award, his Lap 33 pass of Nico Rosberg earned him the FIA 'Action of the Year' award. Not bad for a teenage delinquent.

The season ended with a fourth place in Abu Dhabi and a total of 204 points, fifth in the drivers' championship compared to Daniel Ricciardo's third place with 256 points. Considering Daniel had collected 36 of those before Max arrived, and suffered no DNFs to Max's three retirements, it was closer than the totals suggested.

It was another season where he had surpassed all expectations, re-written the record books (perhaps for all time) and proven his doubters wrong. He had delighted new F1 owners Liberty Media with the kind of on-track action that would bring in a new audience the sport desperately needed. What's more he had found a kindred spirit in fun-loving big bro Daniel Ricciardo, who made all the wacky Red Bull pre-race marketing photo opportunities easier to handle. Things would get a lot tougher in 2017.

THE RACE

FORMULA 1
Brazilian Grand Prix
Autódromo José Carlos Pace, Interlagos, Brazil
16 November, 2016

Wet weather races at Interlagos have a reputation for causing mayhem when 20 Formula 1 cars are unleashed on the old-school circuit. In 2003, running water across the track at Turn 3 created a car park of wrecked machinery behind the Armco, as one car after another misjudged the grip and ran straight on into the barriers, the six cars including world champion Michael Schumacher's Ferrari. The 2016 race was similarly chaotic. At the heart of it was Pirelli's poor-functioning full-wet tyre, which was hardly better than the intermediate, and drivers found themselves aquaplaning and spinning helplessly into the Armco at regular intervals. Grosjean didn't even make it to the grid.

There were five safety cars and two red flags in all. So bad was the wet tyre in these cold conditions, and so variable was the rain, that teams were constantly switching between wets and inters.

LEFT: 'You were getting excited, weren't you?' Max asked engineer Gianpiero Lambiase on team radio after the race. 'You got me a little bit excited,' admitted the unflappable GP. 'Nice job.'

RIGHT: Max celebrates on the Interlagos podium.

FAR RIGHT: Max gave up second place for a shot at the win. Very Verstappen.

On Lap 37 Max was caught out by standing water on the track at the top of the hill and lost the rear end, spearing towards the barriers until he snapped it round with centimetres to spare in what was widely regarded as 'save of the season'. Max admitted to his heart rate going up, but the following lap he was still going a second faster than Nico Rosberg's Mercedes.

In a roll of the dice Verstappen was brought in from second place on Lap 43 for a set of inters to try and chase Lewis down. 'We were going for the win,' explained Christian Horner, 'and we weren't going to achieve that doing the same as Hamilton.'

But the rain started to get worse, and both Max and Daniel Ricciardo were driving on the edge of a big accident using inters. The gamble had failed. Max was asked if he wanted to switch back to wets and he emerged from the pits now back down in 14th place with 15 laps to go.

Verstappen then embarked on a mesmerizing pursuit through the field, charging past a succession of cars, often in places where overtakes are rarely or never made. This included a moment where the Red Bull was almost pushed onto the grass by Felipe Nasr in exactly the same place his father was pushed in 1994. Max made short work of his team-mate, brushed Vettel to the outside at Juncao and finally made an extended pass on future team-mate Sergio Perez for P3 and a podium place. Nobody had been watching the race leader.

'I think we witnessed something very special today,' said Christian Horner. Mercedes boss Toto Wolff was even more complimentary. 'It was really unbelievable driving. Physics are being redefined.'

2017 – Under New Management

Liberty Media opened a pandora's box of opportunity when they took full control of Formula 1 from the start of the 2017 season. Gone was the analog thinking of the old regime. The previous owners had controlled all footage filmed in the paddock, severely limiting the teams', drivers' and sponsors' engagement with social media.

Bernie Ecclestone had relied on TV deals and race hosting fees for his income with a blinkered mindset about new media. The door was now open for drivers to build their profiles with the fans – and the first series of Netflix's *Drive to Survive* was just a year away. It was the perfect opportunity for two media-savvy guys like Max and Daniel to build their following, and for the inventive and agile Red Bull marketing team to promote them.

But if 2016 had seen the great leap forward for Max Verstappen, 2017 would prove to be character building. Jos had a much shorter word for it. The 14th race on the calendar, the Singapore Grand Prix, typified the kind of year Max was enduring. Rain fell on the Marina Bay circuit prior to the race, which meant we were going to get the high drama of our very first wet night race. This would surely suit F1's new 'regenmeister' judging from how Max had handled the 2016 Brazilian GP.

He was starting on the front row next to polesitter Sebastian Vettel, with Daniel Ricciardo right behind in P3. It was the tenth time he'd outqualified his team-mate this year – Max then leading the qualifying battle a decisive 10-4.

As the lights went out Kimi Räikkönen got a flyer of a getaway from fourth on the grid, and was speeding past the Red Bull on the inside and charging for Turn 1 with the momentum to overtake him. Vettel veered across Max's path (not imagining that there might be another Ferrari on the other side of him). Max with nowhere to go, tagged the rear wheel of the Ferrari, spinning it into the path of Sebastian Vettel. Then, as the cars arrived at the corner, the sliding Räikkönen collected Verstappen and pushed him into the innocent bystander Fernando Alonso. Three cars out on the spot, and Vettel out a few corners further on.

Christian Horner was again left rueing what might have been. 'It was enormously frustrating to lose Max at the start of the race, in an incident that quite clearly had nothing to do with him.'

It was Max's seventh retirement in 14 races. In Bahrain he had been sidelined with brake failure, in Spain he had been on the outside when Bottas nudged Räikkönen into him at the first turn. In Canada he retired with electrical problems,

TOP LEFT: Yet again Max gets caught up in somebody else's accident. Vettel cuts sharply across Max's RB13 at the start of the Singapore Grand Prix.

LEFT: Räikkönen and Verstappen exit their damaged cars as the safety car is dispatched in Singapore.

TEAM-MATE STATS

Formula 1 team-mates are an uneasy alliance. No matter how friendly you are with the guy across the garage, a driver's no.1 task is to beat him – and the more you put him in the shade, the more your status rises. That's true even of multiple world champions. In October 2023 when Max was asked what his priorities were; poles, fastest laps etc. he said, 'You always have to beat your team-mate. That is and remains the most important thing. And that's going quite well.' Which of course was an understatement, as Verstappen headed for the greatest points tally of all time, over double his team-mate's score.

2015
Max Verstappen vs Carlos Sainz

	Max Verstappen		Carlos Sainz
QUALIFYING SCORE	9		10
RACES	11		8
PODIUMS	0		0
POINTS TOTAL	49		18
DNFs	4		7
BEST QUALIFYING POSITION	P6		P5
BEST RACE RESULT	P4		P7

2016
Max Verstappen vs Daniel Ricciardo

	Max Verstappen		Daniel Ricciardo
QUALIFYING SCORE	6		10
RACES	7		9
PODIUMS	7		8
POINTS TOTAL	204		256
DNFs	3		0
BEST QUALIFYING POSITION	P2		P1
BEST RACE RESULT	P1		P1

2017
Max Verstappen vs Daniel Ricciardo

	QUALIFYING SCORE	
13		7
	RACES	
11		9
	PODIUMS	
4		9
	POINTS TOTAL	
168		200
	DNFs	
7		6
	BEST QUALIFYING POSITION	
P2		P3
	BEST RACE RESULT	
P1		P1

2018
Max Verstappen vs Daniel Ricciardo

	QUALIFYING SCORE	
15		6
	RACES	
16		5
	PODIUMS	
11		2
	POINTS TOTAL	
249		170
	DNFs	
3		8
	BEST QUALIFYING POSITION	
P2		P1
	BEST RACE RESULT	
P1		P1

2019
Max Verstappen vs Pierre Gasly

	QUALIFYING SCORE	
11		1
	RACES	
11		1
	PODIUMS	
5		0
	POINTS TOTAL	
181		63
	DNFs	
0		1
	BEST QUALIFYING POSITION	
P1		P4
	BEST RACE RESULT	
P1		P4

in Azerbaijan (a race that Ricciardo won) he'd qualified five places in front of Daniel but lost oil pressure and was forced to stop the car. He qualified on the third row of the grid in Austria but got bogged down at the start and swallowed up by the midfield runners before they all piled into the melee of Spielberg Turn 1. Again he was on the outside when Fernando Alonso was struck by a car spearing up the inside, missing its braking point. Alonso's McLaren cannoned into Max's Red Bull putting both cars out. Guilty party Daniil Kvyat in the Toro Rosso torpedo was able to continue.

There were hopes of a good result in front of home fans at the Belgian Grand Prix, but a power unit failure after only seven laps meant another morale-sapping DNF. Then came his disappointment in Singapore. He might have been trouncing the Honey Badger in the qualifying battle, but after the first 14 races Daniel had scored seven podiums, including a win. Max had a solitary third place from the Chinese Grand Prix. Worse than that, he'd put in jeopardy his good relationship with Daniel after an incident in Budapest.

Monaco and the Hungaroring represented the two places where Red Bull might predict a victory in 2017. The Renault RE17 engines had now been branded TAG-Heuer for sponsorship purposes, but it didn't make them any faster. Monaco had turned out to be a Ferrari 1–2, with Daniel third and Max fifth. The Hungarian Grand Prix was also less power dependent and could be the chance for the team's best points haul of the year. As if to cement this idea, Dietrich Mateschitz turned up to watch the race, one of the handful he would attend.

Max got a great start from fifth on the grid, sweeping round the outside of Valtteri Bottas into Turn 1, and looked to be heading for third place into Turn 2. But then he got boxed in behind Kimi Räikkönen. That loss of momentum allowed Bottas to escape and team-mate Daniel Ricciardo to slip past on the inside. Heading for Turn 2 Max looked like he wanted a place back straight away – a throwback to his old karting days. Coming from way too far back he locked his brakes and slid hard into his team-mate's left sidepod, puncturing the radiator. Ricciardo was out on the spot. 'Is that who I thought it was?' he inquired on team radio, '****ing sore loser!'

For a man who never emitted an angry word, this was more dramatic than Sebastian Vettel's expletive-laden Sochi rant. In a Sky Sports interview a furious Ricciardo called Verstappen 'amateur' and said he made a 'very poor mistake'. But by Monday morning, a more sanguine Daniel indicated that he'd talked it out with Max. 'Yesterday was hard to take,' he wrote on Twitter. 'You build up all day

TOP LEFT: Parking the car would become a familiar routine for Max in 2017. It started in the Barcelona test.

TOP RIGHT: At least Max could indulge himself with some big air on his Red Bull jet ski when he got home.

LEFT: Max slides into Daniel at Turn 2 of the Hungaroring. Their second major impact, a year later, would effectively end the bromance.

for those couple hours of racing and then it's gone like that. Max apologized to me after the race and we spoke one on one, away from media or anyone. The situation was handled and taken care of in the right way to move forward. Lights go out again in four weeks.'

For a man who doesn't like to apologize, Max was conciliatory. The 10-second penalty he got for the avoidable accident denied him the chance of a win or even a podium place. 'It's never my intention to hit anyone but especially not my team-mate,' Max said, 'and especially with the relationship I have with Daniel which is very good.' The next time they would clash he would be unrepentant.

For now, things carried on as they were. Proof of a long-term friendship is evident from the *Whatever It Takes* documentary where Daniel hijacks Max for a night out on his 22nd birthday with some of the Monaco crew, including Pierre Gasly. The birthday boy has more than a couple of cheeky beers on a riotous night out and the film crew is there with him as he staggers back to his Monaco apartment, scrabbling for the key under the mat.

As it transpired, the Singapore Grand Prix was the turning point of Max's season. Next time out in Malaysia, at his happy hunting ground of Sepang, he won. In fact the Red Bull drivers' fortunes were completely reversed for the last six races of the year, with Max finishing in the top five in all of them, while Daniel retired three times. Max added another win in Mexico after a robust-but-fair opening corner where he refused to give way to Vettel and the pair made brief

BOTTOM LEFT: Max and Daniel talked their Hungarian GP incident through, and normal service was soon resumed.

BELOW: Max wins his second grand prix in Malaysia and suddenly his season is back on track.

RIGHT: With Daniel finishing on the podium in Sepang there was double reason for celebration. Max would win again in Mexico, three races later.

contact as they ran side by side through the tight first chicane. Tom Petty's 1989 single 'I Won't Back Down' should be the soundtrack for most Verstappen overtaking moves.

At season end Max had scored 168 points to Daniel's 200 and they had finished fifth and sixth in the drivers' table, and stayed friends. Daniel had scored nine podiums with a single win, while Max made it four podiums and two wins. Things would not be so easy between them in 2018.

This is the last time Max would be beaten by a team-mate over the course of a Formula 1 season.

THE RACE

FORMULA 1
United States Grand Prix
Circuit of the Americas, Austin, Texas
22 October, 2017

Max had never finished on the podium of the USGP, though he had come close for Toro Rosso in 2014. It didn't look like he was going to do any better in 2017 after taking an engine penalty that relegated his starting position to 16th having qualified just behind Daniel Ricciardo in sixth.

When the race started underneath a sunny Texan sky, Max set off towards the points positions with a typical Verstappen charge. Keeping clear of trouble, he had passed Sergio Perez's Force India for P10 by the third lap. By Lap 10 he had used the DRS system to overtake Esteban Ocon and take sixth place, his original Q3 position.

Red Bull had started him on the hard tyres, so Max was able to run much longer in the first stint than his competitors and even temporarily led the race before diving in for soft tyres. He recommenced his charge forwards, now catching the cars in front at 1.5 seconds a lap. With team-mate Ricciardo out of the race following an oil pressure problem Max set his sights on third place.

Sebastian Vettel and Hamilton were too far up the road but he might still be able to pick off Bottas and Kimi Räikkönen, the Ferrari having to lift and coast to save fuel. He managed to elbow Bottas aside on Lap 52 out of 56, moving up to fourth, and on the final part of the last lap positioned himself on the gearbox of 'the Ice Man'.

The Ferrari driver had kept him at bay on the long back straight where the majority of moves are made; all looked good for Kimi. But Max made his superior late-race grip count by sticking his Red Bull up the inside at Turn 16. To make the move and avoid the possibility of Räikkönen clattering into him he skipped across the apex kerbing, taking all four wheels marginally off track.

The crowd celebrated wildly; a voluble Christian Horner came on team radio as he crossed the finish line in P3 seconds later: 'Max Verstappen, you are brilliant! What an overtake!'

But the move on Räikkönen had been spotted by driver steward Mika Salo (an ex-Ferrari driver and fellow Finn). The penalty for leaving the track and gaining an advantage was five seconds added to his time, demoting him to P4.

RIGHT: Pumped with adrenaline, Max is about ten minutes away from some very disappointing news.

Max had been sitting in the cool-down room waiting to go on stage for his first USGP podium appearance. His mum, his dad and his sister Victoria were down there in the crowd, expecting him to walk out, when Kimi Räikkönen entered the green room. It was only then, in the glare of the TV cameras, that Max learned the penalty decision and that he would not be getting to spray champagne.

In the heat of disappointment, with emotions running high, he referred to the stewards in media interviews afterwards as something worse than idiots – but it was a decision he had to accept and comments he needed to apologize for. Which he did. But the drive had shown a US audience his true swashbuckling style.

ABOVE: The Halo was
an important addition to
open-wheel racing in
2018.

2018 – The Year of Living Dangerously

The ambitions of both Red Bull drivers rested on the engine unit behind them. Chief Technical Officer Adrian Newey is unquestionably the best Formula 1 designer of his generation, perhaps of all time, but no matter how agile or aerodynamically slippery he could make the RB14, their 2018 contender still relied on a Renault RE18 engine. Of the available power units it was deemed to be the third quickest of the four engine suppliers, though Honda were rapidly catching up.

McLaren's two world champion drivers, Jenson Button and Fernando Alonso, had endured a miserable time with their Honda-powered car, proving that you can have all the talent in the world behind the wheel, but if the car is constantly parked at the side of the track smoking, your career is going nowhere. Alonso drove home the point repeatedly in team radio messages and once sunbathing in a marshal's chair at Interlagos. Button took a sabbatical in 2018.

McLaren switched to Renault engines for 2018 and the Red Bull organization saw an opportunity to install Honda engines in the Toro Rosso STR13. Christian Horner and Adrian Newey were keen to get an invested engine supplier. Always on their mind was a visit they'd made to see the top boss of Renault at the beginning of the hybrid era. 'We went to see Carlos Ghosn to try to put pressure on him to up the budget,' Newey revealed in a Beyond the Grid podcast. 'Ghosn's reply was, "Well, I have no interest in Formula 1. I'm only in it because my marketing people say I should be." That was such a depressing place to be.'

Red Bull took the first steps of extricating themselves from a loveless marriage with the Toro Rosso change. Franz Tost supervised a successful integration with

ABOVE RIGHT: Max and Seb ended up at 90 degrees to the racing line in China.

Honda in 2018 which paved the way for the senior team taking their engines a year later, in 2019. But for now Red Bull would still be running the TAG-Heuer badged Renault.

As the cars lined up on the grid in Melbourne for the opening round it was clear to see that all the cars had undergone a major change. Gone were the shark's fin engine covers, more importantly in had come the new 'halo' cockpit protection device, integral to all FIA-approved series going forward. It would save F1 drivers' lives from that season onwards. Including Max's rival in 2021.

There was no major change in the Red Bull result, though, with Max barely outqualifying Daniel, and Daniel outracing Max – fourth and sixth in Australia was not spectacular, but the cars had been reliable. Which is more than can be said for the following race, Bahrain, where the Red Bull mechanics were packing

up the garage after three laps, Max out with a transmission issue, Daniel with an electrical problem.

In China their fortunes turned round completely with a well-timed strategy call from the team. Equipped with fresher tyres after a safety car had been called just as the leaders passed the pit entry, Ricciardo and Verstappen set about picking off the cars in front who had missed the trick. Max was leading his team-mate at this point but tried to rush his way past Hamilton too early, ran wide, and was overtaken by Daniel. They both set about the two Mercedes and two Ferraris in front, Daniel proving to everyone that he was indeed the master of the late brakers. On the podium, winner's trophy in hand, he told Martin Brundle, 'Sometimes you gotta lick the stamp and send it!' before performing the now obligatory shoey.

Max should have been alongside in P2, but a clumsy overtaking move on Vettel (who else) at the hairpin saw Max punt his Red Bull into the Ferrari and both cars perform some synchronized spinning, losing places for both and gaining Max a 10-second penalty from the stewards. Max, forever learning, went and found Vettel afterwards to apologize. 'I could see him struggling on the tyres and tried to brake late into the corner. I locked the rears a bit and hit him. That was of course my fault,' he admitted in the media pen.

Vettel, despite getting a huge dent in his championship challenge, was gracious in return. 'I think he realized he was wrong,' said Sebastian. 'We were both lucky to continue. However, I appreciated the fact he came to me straightway because that's the way to solve things like this, face to face.'

So, this was the backdrop as the teams headed for Baku and the Azerbaijan Grand Prix. Max might have been expected to make amends for losing the team points – that's not how he saw it. Right from the start the two Red Bulls were rubbing tyres in a bid to get in front of each other. Sky F1 commentator David Croft called it as Max made another robust move: 'Daniel Ricciardo has to give him space or, not for the first time this afternoon, the two Red Bulls would have hit each other. They've hit each other once, they could have hit each other three times

ABOVE: Team boss Christian Horner rarely loses control of his emotions, but he was very angry in Baku.

LEFT: No contact this time round as the two Red Bull drivers rub tyres and exchange places going into Turn 1 at the 2018 Azerbaijan Grand Prix.

quite frankly. Verstappen is in no mood to yield to his team-mate or accept that his team-mate has got past him. It's great racing, but if you are Christian Horner you are not enjoying this for one second!' He was right.

Daniel got past Max at the end of the start/finish straight, but then the pit-stops reversed the order so it was Groundhog Day all over again. On Lap 40, Daniel was fast approaching Max into the same overtaking spot right in front of the pits, dummied right, Max moved right, then Daniel dived left and Max swerved left. Ricciardo was committed to his line and had nowhere to go. His Red Bull slammed into the back of Verstappen and both cars showered sparks as they skeetered out of control into the run-off zone. An instant double DNF.

Back in the debrief room Horner took on the disappointed headmaster role and laid into them for putting their own interests in front of the team. He wanted them both at the factory in Milton Keynes next week to apologize to each department for wrecking all their hard work. Max affected youthful nonchalance to the telling off, but for Ricciardo it was harder to swallow. He didn't appreciate being addressed 'like a naughty kid for something I don't think I was at fault for'. It was a view shared by some in the pitlane.

'It was 70 per cent Verstappen's fault, 30 per cent Ricciardo's,' said Niki Lauda. 'Ricciardo was aggressive, but when the other guy chops across him like that, it leaves him nowhere to go.'

Others thought Daniel would never have got his car turned in and would have gone sailing into the run-off had Max's car not been there. Toto Wolff believed a clash was inevitable. 'You cannot have guard dogs in the car and expect them to behave like puppies,' said the Mercedes boss.

The guard dogs behaved themselves in Spain with Max scoring a podium, despite losing parts of his front wing against a lapped Lance Stroll. Then it was on to Monaco, where Red Bull entertained high hopes of a win. Would it be Max or would it be Daniel?

From the moment he headed Free Practice 1 it was Daniel in charge. He was fastest in all three practices – and most importantly, didn't end FP3 in the barriers.

LEFT: Yet again, the Swimming Pool exit barriers at Monaco claim Max's car.

RIGHT: The FIA press conference in Canada where Max issued his 'headbutt' threat to the press.

Max's repeat accident (from 2016) at the Swimming Pool exit ruled his car out of qualifying while Daniel took pole position. In the race Ricciardo had to manage an ERS-K failure that robbed him of a power boost from Lap 28, but still managed to take the win. Max was ninth and had to grin and watch the traditional post-race pool party as Ricciardo took the celebratory dive into the rooftop swimming pool of Red Bull's 'Energy Station'.

In Canada things weren't so jolly. Journalists had been totting up the number of crashes, damaging excursions and collisions Max had been involved in since the start of the season. The BBC's Andrew Benson totted up six incidents in six races. At the pre-race press conference, when asked by another journalist why he crashed so much, the Jos side of Max's personality came to the surface. 'I get tired of the questions,' deadpanned Max. 'If I get a few more, I might headbutt someone.'

It wasn't the greatest of PR responses and Max articulated his attitude a lot better in later interviews, the Sophie side of his personality shining through. 'I am happy how I am. Of course I am not happy with how the season has gone so far,' he explained.'I know pretty well what went wrong, I took my lessons from that and have some great people around me who can always support me. I don't think I need outside help. I have shown in the past years I know how to do it.'

Max confessed to a lack of interest in poring over the previous races to see where things had gone wrong. 'I never really look back because you can't

TOP LEFT: Ocon, in the Force India, tries to unlap himself, with disastrous consequences for the race leader.

ABOVE: The Oranje Army were out in force at the Red Bull Ring to watch Max claim his fourth GP win.

change that. The things you can change and influence is what's ahead and that is what I always try to do.'

True to his word, he never did look back in 2018. In Canada he qualified third and finished third behind Sebastian Vettel and Valtteri Bottas. Apart from Silverstone (15th – brakes) and Budapest (DNF – power unit) the lowest he'd come would be fifth. An impressive haul.

At season end he'd amassed 11 podiums, taking wins in Austria, in front of the massed ranks of the Oranje grandstands and a repeat win in Mexico. It should have been three wins, except an old sparring partner from his European

Formula 3 days got in the way at the Brazilian Grand Prix. Ocon.

On a day when Red Bull's tyre wear was infinitely superior to Ferrari and Mercedes, Max was driving away from Lewis Hamilton's fading W09, the Brit's engineers warning him that exhaust temperatures were going off the dial and he'd have to drop engine modes. A first win for Max in Brazil seemed totally in the bag. Until Esteban Ocon came into the picture.

Driving for Force India, the Frenchman had just switched to a set of supersofts, a much quicker tyre than Verstappen was running. After following Max for a couple of laps and realizing he was faster, he decided to unlap himself on Lap 43. Coming into the braking zone for Turn 1, the Senna Esses, he showed his nose on the outside and was momentarily in front of the Red Bull before they dropped left. Max went straight for the second apex, not realizing that Ocon was seriously trying to pass him and still there and the Force India clunked into him, spinning him round and damaging bodywork. Max had to settle for P2.

'Mate, I don't know what to say,' consoled his engineer Gianpiero Lambiase on the slowdown lap, 'I do not know what to say about that.'

Max seemed relatively in control of his emotions. 'Yeah, I know what to say. I hope now I can't find him in the paddock, because then his...' at which point team radio bleeped out the thing he was going to do next involving Esteban.

ABOVE: Christian Horner presides over a heartfelt farewell to Danny Ric at Red Bull HQ.

ABOVE: Daniel would be a hard act to follow. Next up was Pierre Gasly, photographed here with Max at a pre-season event in Tokyo.

Unfortunately he did find him in the paddock quite soon after, queuing up to be weighed. The smirk on Ocon's face ignited Max's anger and the 'Jos side' took over, Verstappen started pushing Ocon aggressively and had to be restrained. Given the provocation and the adrenaline rush all drivers experience after a race, it's surprising it doesn't happen more often. It made a dramatic episode for *Drive to Survive*, but Formula 1 drivers aren't allowed to behave like footballers and the FIA gave him two days of community service.

In contrast to Verstappen's impressive second half of the season, Ricciardo failed to score another podium finish after Monaco. In early August he made an announcement that rocked the driver market. He was leaving Red Bull.

He had been a Red Bull driver since his Junior days in 2008 and now he was leaving for Renault. Christian Horner could hardly believe it, or the team he was going to. He was convinced Daniel would stay. Reports swirled round that he had turned down £20 million to stay and drive alongside Max Verstappen. But after Azerbaijan Ricciardo could see the direction of travel. If he were ever going to be world champion he would have to elbow his way past Max Verstappen and that didn't seem possible with Helmut Marko in Max's corner. Verstappen had lost his second team-mate, with Pierre Gasly promoted from Toro Rosso.

2019 – Pierre Pressure

The next two team-mates off Red Bull's conveyor belt of talent in 2019 had a mountain to climb. By now one of the fastest learners ever to step into a grand prix car, Max had four seasons of experience under his belt. It wasn't all about learning the nuances of the circuits or perfecting the overtakes, Max had the knowledge that couldn't be replicated by a simulator. It was all about tyres. The ability to manage degradation across Pirelli's range of tyres was something to be learned, with tarmac surface, track temperature, understeer, oversteer all computed in.

A perfect example came from the 2023 Japanese Grand Prix, where rookie Oscar Piastri put his McLaren on the front row alongside Max and ahead of team-mate Lando Norris.

At a circuit he'd never driven before this was impressive stuff. But that was single-lap pace. Suzuka is a high-degradation circuit and in the race the more experienced Norris passed and drove away from him. As Oscar admitted afterwards, 'The only way you can learn is by just doing the races.'

BELOW: The Aston Martin-sponsored Red Bull team produced special 007 race suits for the British GP and posed their drivers in the Bond DB6. Pierre was at the wheel, when in reality he was in the ejector seat.

In 2019 first Pierre Gasly and subsequently Alex Albon could occasionally get close to Max, but they couldn't challenge him in races the way that Ricciardo had applied pressure. Daniel had five seasons' experience of racing, of adapting to Pirelli tyres, before he had to deal with Max – Pierre had just over one. Alex Albon had only completed 12 races for Toro Rosso in 2019 before he was thrust into the lion's den of the senior team, alongside Red Bull's No.1 driver (who also had a lion on his helmet). Helmut Marko had seen enough of Gasly after 12 races and relegated him to Toro Rosso after the Hungarian Grand Prix, the Frenchman deemed to be unable to take the pressure.

Not that Max was intimidating his team-mates with Vettel-like attention to telemetry. Alex Albon had known him since their karting days and they got on well. 'He's got a lot of self-confidence, which you need, but not arrogance,' Alex told the Red Bull podcast. 'When it was time for qualifying or Free Practice 3, I was getting ready, looking at data, and he was playing FIFA or Call of Duty. I admire it, I wish I could be that relaxed.'

BELOW: The start of the 2019 Monaco Grand Prix and Max plays it cautious into St Dévote.

THE RACE

FORMULA 1
Austrian Grand Prix
Red Bull Ring, Spielberg, Austria
30 June, 2019

The massed ranks of the Oranje Army had assembled for their annual Austrian holiday in the Styrian hills. This year the crowds dressed in orange were bigger than ever, packing out grandstands, and they had come to the Red Bull Ring with one thing on their mind (apart from partying all day and most of the night), to see Max on the podium.

It had been another Silver Arrows benefit year, but the Mercedes engine didn't work so well at 660m of altitude, allowing Ferrari to get a foot in the door – and maybe Red Bull too...?

Charles Leclerc qualified on pole and Sebastian Vettel would have been alongside him had Seb not suffered a mechanical problem in Q3 – Max was on the second row in P3, ideally placed for a charge. Then disaster. As the lights went out, Max's Red Bull bogged down and he was slow away, overtaken by team-mate Gasly, and had fallen back to eighth place at Turn 1.

Nobody realized at the time that his poor start was an inadvertent tactical masterstroke.

Starting so far back, Ferrari viewed the two Mercedes cars as their main opposition for the win. So when Valtteri Bottas, running second, came in for his first stop, Ferrari reacted and brought race leader Charles Leclerc in to cover off the undercut. A close inspection of Leclerc's soft tyres showed he could have run for many more laps – which is exactly what Max did to get back in the game.

Verstappen steadily picked off drivers, including Hamilton (in the pits, after his late pit-stop), Vettel and Bottas. There was mounting excitement in the crowd as they realized that the win might just be possible. Leclerc was running out of tyres after stopping so early, Max's tyres had run 10 fewer laps.

Suddenly there was trouble. Just before he caught Bottas the Red Bull slowed. 'I'm losing power!' Max yelled to his engineer. With a quick adjustment to correct a faulty exhaust sensor, he was back on the gas. Having cleared Bottas he was just 5.5 seconds behind Leclerc with 13 laps to go.

Both drivers radioed back and were given the green light to up their engine modes. With Honda's vice-principal attending the race, Red Bull's home grand prix, Max got to turn his Honda engine up to Mode 11. It might have shortened the engine's lifespan, but hell, this was an opportunity. Roared on by the crowd he closed the Ferrari down.

With six laps to go Verstappen was within DRS range. On Lap 68 his old karting adversary was defending expertly; Max got ahead through Turn 3, but Charles outdragged him in the second DRS zone and was back in front by Turn 4. It was edge-of-the-plastic-seat stuff.

On Lap 69 of 71, Verstappen left his braking even later as he dived for the

LEFT: Max's weekend got off to a bad start when he crashed in second practice.

BELOW: A conciliatory handshake from one of his pitcrew as they go off to recover the stricken car.

inside of Turn 3, this time leaving Leclerc even less space on exit. Wheels banged. Leclerc refused to yield and the Red Bull nudged/ushered the Ferrari out onto the kerbing causing it to lose momentum. The grandstands were a blur of orange hands punching the air.

'What the hell was that?' Leclerc yelled over team radio, mostly for the benefit of the stewards. 'He pushed me off the track!'

'It's hard racing,' Max replied after the race. 'Otherwise we have to stay home. If those things aren't allowed in racing, then what's the point of being in Formula 1?'

Max took the win to send his Oranje Army wild and cue intense celebrations in the Red Bull garage. It was Max's sixth grand prix win, more importantly it was Honda's first F1 win since 2006, their first since the disastrous return with McLaren in 2015. On the podium Max smiled and pointed to the Honda badge, while below him grown men wept.

ABOVE: Max's fans were out in force at Spielberg. Could he make it two Austrian GPs in a row...?

RIGHT: On the podium Max points to the Honda logo. This was a win that mattered.

The new Honda engine unit for 2019 had immediately brought results. Max scored his best ever result in Australia with a third place, while Gasly failed to get out of Q1, qualifying in 17th and finishing down in 12th.

Verstappen would finish no lower than fifth until the Belgian Grand Prix in September – with no retirements along the way. It was quite a turn-around from 2018. In Monaco he revealed the new Max 2.0 by qualifying third on the grid and going wheel to wheel with Bottas towards the first corner, St Dévote – where he'd had the Grosjean accident in 2015 – and backed off, even though he had the inside line. For the last 20 laps of the race he was pushing leader Lewis Hamilton hard, including a friendly nerf to Hamilton's rear tyre coming into the chicane, but could find no way past. He was second across the line, just metres away from the Mercedes, but was demoted to fourth with a five-second penalty. An unsafe release in the pit-stops, when the Red Bull team had launched him into the path of Valtteri Bottas, denied him the podium.

Verstappen was not frustrated by the turn of events. 'The whole race, following that closely in the dirty air through the high-speed corners, is not that easy around here, but I had a fun race. Of course I would have liked to have been on the podium but if we look at the pace and performance, we were strong.'

In Austria, Round 9 of the championship, they were stronger still. The ranks of Verstappen fans were swelling from year to year, creating a festival atmosphere in the hills above Spielberg, with very few of them drinking Heineken 0.0. They were partying into the small hours after Max scored the first Red Bull-Honda win, a significant milestone (see Greatest Races page 152). Jos Verstappen was celebrating too. He had been a Honda test driver, recruited to be part of the

TOP LEFT: Kvyat and Verstappen on the podium in Germany, the day after he became a father.

TOP RIGHT: Max and Alex Albon ask each other some set questions at Monza before the 2019 Italian Grand Prix. And Max says he doesn't enjoy marketing...

RIGHT: Spreading the F1 word: the Red Bulls parked up outside Grauman's Chinese Theatre as part of the F1 Hollywood Festival in October 2019.

Japanese team's abandoned entry to F1 in 2000, axed after the death of Harvey Postlethwaite. 'I really enjoyed it for the Honda people because they went through such a difficult time with McLaren,' Jos recalled.

Two races later he did it again. The German Grand Prix was a wet race run in changeable conditions with cars spinning off the track in the wet, and cars spinning off on slicks when they strayed outside the dry line. Nobody completed the race without some kind of off-track excursion and Max executed a neat 360-degree, impactless pirouette, on his way to victory.

Daniil Kvyat, back in the Toro Rosso team after a year's sabbatical as a Ferrari reserve driver, came home third in the race. Asked about Kvyat's podium performance, Christian Horner couldn't hide his joy for his former driver who was

celebrating the birth of a daughter, Penelope, with girlfriend Kelly Piquet.

'Unbelievable,' purred Horner, 'He should have more kids! I'm so pleased for him. He's kept his head down, he's fought his way back into the Red Bull programme ... For him to become a father last night and be on the podium today – it was a very mature drive by him.'

In the winner's press conference, Kvyat reminded everyone that it had been 11 years since the last Toro Rosso podium: 'I think everyone is very happy today and we have to be happy. From my side of course I would dedicate this podium to my girlfriend Kelly and to my daughter.' He and Max had previously joked about receiving Helmut Marko's early morning calls. Max nudged him, 'Now, you have to wake up at like, every three hours...' He could not have imagined that in less than two years he would be performing step-fatherly duties.

There would be one more win in 2019, at Interlagos, and another first for Max. He had not won from pole position since his Formula 3 days and the Brazilian Grand Prix was a commanding performance at a race Lewis Hamilton likes to call his own. Late in the grand prix, the Brit had clattered into Alex Albon's Red Bull in an ill-timed desperate lunge for second place, ruining both their races.

Without the Mercedes battering, Alex would have finished no lower than sixth place in all his races. It looked as though this Toro Rosso graduate could be the perfect foil for Verstappen as Honda refined their engine for 2020.

LEFT: Drivers line up for a photo opportunity at the start of 2020 testing in Barcelona.

RIGHT: Waiting for the season to start in the Melbourne paddock.

2020 Emergency Measures

The 2020 season started in Melbourne, Australia, with an FIA press conference for drivers scheduled on Thursday 12 March. The problems of Covid-19 were looming large. US President Donald Trump had just closed the national borders to flights from Europe and McLaren and Haas were having team members tested for Covid. Asked directly if he thought the Australian Grand Prix should go ahead Lewis Hamilton said it was for others to decide, but frankly he was shocked that they were there when other sports, such as the NBA in America, had been suspended.

When the McLaren team member tested positive for Covid, the team withdrew from the race. Formula 1 team principals convened a meeting. It was a unanimous decision that the race should be cancelled.

And then the world of sport came to a halt with the first global Covid lockdown.

When Max moved out of home, Jos always said that he was never worried about leaving him to his own devices in Monaco because his manager, Raymond, lived there and could keep an eye on him.

So now Max and his manager were separated from the world while a global solution for the pandemic was sought. In truth, Max was set up for a long period

at home. He had everything he needed in the apartment, his gym equipment, his simulator where he could indulge his love for Esports with Team Redline. And his good friend Lando Norris was just round the corner, should limited socializing be allowed.

Helpful as ever, Helmut Marko had been busy thinking up a scheme to protect his drivers for when the season reconvened – because surely it would...

Speaking on Austrian television he revealed that he wanted to put Max and his Red Bull-contracted fellow drivers in a 'Covid camp' to catch the disease early and gain immunity. 'The idea was to organize a camp where we could bridge what is mentally and physically somewhat dead time,' said Marko.

'And that would be the ideal time for the infection to come. They are all strong young men in really good health. That way they would be prepared whenever the action starts – ready for what will probably be a very tough championship.'

ABOVE: The reset button for the 2020 calendar sent cars to the Red Bull Ring in Austria for Round 1. Max retired from the race with an electronics issue.

ABOVE RIGHT: Helmut Marko and Christian Horner talk with Max in Austria as Formula 1 learns to adapt to a new way of working.

It was a story reported on 30 March and Christian Horner defended his boss by pointing out that at that stage in the pandemic, neither Marko nor the medical world had gauged the severity of the disease. While Helmut dreamed of racing again, the Red Bull team were heavily involved in 'Project Pitlane'. With their fast-build engineering capacity, seven Formula 1 teams in the UK were signed up to develop ventilators to help coronavirus sufferers with the idea of reverse engineering existing medical devices.

As the world gradually learned how to protect itself, Formula 1 reshaped its calendar to resurrect a season that at one stage looked lost. In August 2019 Formula One Management had been delighted to announce, 'An unprecedented 22 grands prix' for its 70th anniversary season. Along the way there will be seven back-to-back race weekends and two exciting new additions.' The Vietnamese Grand Prix in April became a terminal casualty and Team Verstappen soon realized that they would not get to race at Zandvoort for the resurrected Dutch GP in May.

Neither could the Oranje Army carry out their annual invasion of Austria as the first races at the Red Bull Ring, Hungaroring and Silverstone were run for the television cameras only, without spectators. Or, as one pitlane cynic remarked, 'like the Bahrain Grand Prix for the first five years'.

Employing a series of strictly controlled 'bubbles' the teams stayed in Austria for two races starting in July, nipped across the border to Budapest, and then moved home to Silverstone for two races in August. The success of the bubble system can be judged by the number of drivers who missed grands prix with

Covid across the season; only Perez, Stroll and Lewis Hamilton had to sit out races.

Max continued his good form from 2019 with a win in the fifth race of the year at Silverstone. Although the season hadn't started well with a retirement from the Austrian Grand Prix with an electrical problem on Lap 11. 'I suddenly just lost power, drive, got into anti-stall and stuff,' said Verstappen after the race. 'I don't know what the problem is yet... We'll find out but of course it's not how you want to start.'

After that, if Verstappen finished a race, he would be on the podium all the way through to the Turkish Grand Prix in mid-November. Lewis Hamilton was untouchable in 2020, but Max would have easily clinched second place from Valtteri Bottas had five retirements not taken him out of the equation. Though, as we have learned, Max doesn't treasure second places.

He was able to celebrate his first win at Silverstone for the 70th Anniversary Grand Prix (the first ever F1 race had taken place at the old bomber training base in 1950) in reasonably calm fashion after Mercedes blistered their tyres, and more importantly, at the final race in Abu Dhabi. Max's win at the Yas Marina circuit was a marker for the tumultuous season ahead.

Verstappen qualified his RB16 on pole, only the third pole of his career and, significantly, the first time since 2013 that Mercedes had not taken pole in Abu Dhabi. In the race, he simply drove away from both Mercedes cars, finishing fifteen seconds ahead of Bottas, with Lewis, returning after Covid, in third place.

'It shows how good their car is,' said Hamilton. 'Alex (Albon) was right behind me and that hasn't been the case really for most of the year. It shows they've made progress, Alex has made progress, and I think that's really good for the sport.'

Unfortunately Alex hadn't made good enough progress for Helmut.

Max was fairly nonchalant about his tenth victory. 'To be able to win the last race is a good boost for everyone and a good motivation for the team going into winter,' he told Sky TV. 'I hope next season we can be more competitive from the start.' If he had been told that three years later he would be interviewed on the same spot with 54 wins to his name, as a three-times world champion, he wouldn't have believed it.

TOP LEFT AND ABOVE: Max celebrates his win at the 70th Anniversary Grand Prix, one of two races held at Silverstone.

LEFT: The season finale in Abu Dhabi provided Max with his second win of 2020, but sadly it was also the final Red Bull race for team-mate Alex Albon.

A FIGHT TO THE FINISH

PREVIOUS PAGE:
Defensive driving
from Lewis Hamilton
in Portimao, Portugal.

LEFT: A new season
and a new team-
mate. Max and
Checo line up for
some promotional
filming for the 'reveal'
of the 2022 prototype
at Silverstone.

In the 2020 Sakhir Grand Prix, driving for Force India, 'Checo' Perez ('in Mexico all Sergios are nicknamed Checo') drove through the field from last to first and scored an unlikely yet impressive victory. He was out of a job for 2021 with Sebastian Vettel arriving to take his place at the soon-to-be-renamed Racing Point team. The Mexican had long been admired for his ability to eke out long stints on Pirelli tyres and Helmut Marko saw him as the perfect 'alternative strategy' driver for his beloved Max.

Alex Albon had already been told the bad news when the Red Bull press release hit media inboxes on 18 December.

'Current driver Alex Albon remains an important member of the team and takes on the role of Red Bull Racing Test and Reserve Driver with a key focus on 2022 development, simulator work and tyre testing,' the press release informed. Christian Horner said: 'Alex is a valued member of the team and we thought long and hard about this decision.'

Horner is a master of the poker face in media interviews, highly adept at delivering the company line whether he believes in it or not. There were those in the paddock who thought it was Marko making snap driver decisions and Christian having to find context for them.

The fact that management needed to look outside the Red Bull Junior Programme was both an admission that the scheme wasn't working and an acknowledgement that Max's performances were overawing his team-mates.

Red Bull got an early-season boost when the FIA decided to outlaw Mercedes' highly advanced Dual Axis Steering system (DAS) that optimized grip for the front wheels. The FIA had already handed Mercedes' high-rake rivals (cars such as Red Bull, with a high rear end and a low front end) an

advantage by requiring teams to nominate the areas they could develop in 2021. Once the teams had lodged the technical documents, the FIA changed the rules regarding floor dimensions and the lower bargeboard area, which affected the low-rake teams (such as Mercedes), who were then locked into the two changes they were allowed. Neither of which involved the floor.

Even so, after four races Lewis had won three of them, Max muscling his way past Hamilton on the opening lap of the Emilia Romagna Grand Prix at Imola for his first win of 2021. It was a true statement of intent from Verstappen. He had been made to surrender a winning position in Bahrain for overtaking with four wheels off the track as Hamilton pushed him wide. Imola had been Max's revenge – and set the tone for 2021. (See Greatest Races page 170)

The not-so-good news from Imola was that Max's new wingman was hopelessly adrift, Perez tangling with Yuki Tsunoda's Alpha Tauri (the rebranded Toro Rosso) and finishing down in 11th place.

Next up was Monaco. Cancelled in 2020 because of Covid, Max had hit the barriers more than most in the principality, with his best finish a fourth place in 2019. He had yet to get on the podium in his adopted home race. But this was going to be a race that favoured the high-rake cars such as Ferrari and Red Bull, who could crank

ABOVE: Max outdrags Lewis Hamilton to the first corner at Imola and nudges him helpfully over the kerbing.

ABOVE RIGHT: For once Monaco proved to be a happy hunting ground and Verstappen took his first win at F1's most prestigious race.

RIGHT: Girlfriend Kelly Piquet wasn't waiting for him to get his HANS device off, once he got back.

up the downforce by elevating the back end of the car. Mercedes had no such scope in their set-up window.

As if to prove the point, Charles Leclerc put his Ferrari on provisional pole during Q3 and then crashed at speed on the Swimming Pool exit, exactly the same place Max had crashed in 2016 and 2018. Unlike 2006, when Michael Schumacher had put his Ferrari on pole then brought qualifying to an ugly end with the kind of spin not even a rookie would make, this looked a genuine mistake by the Monegasque.

Max was following behind and saw the red flags as he sped through the tunnel. He had made a mistake on his previous lap but was still sitting in P2.

'Leclerc's in the wall at Turn 16,' Gianpiero Lambiase, his engineer, told him. Max let rip. He knew his aborted lap was good enough for pole. 'Yep,' confirmed GP, '1.5 seconds up by Turn 8.'

THE RACE

FORMULA 1
Emilia Romagna Grand Prix
Autodromo Internazionale Enzo e Dino Ferrari, Imola, Italy
18 April, 2021

The 2021 Emilia Romagna Grand Prix had everything you could ask for from a Formula 1 race – apart from spectators. Run in the early days of Covid recovery it was still too soon to welcome back fans to the grandstands, which was a pity because the second race of the 2021 season provided great drama.

Cars started with intermediate tyres on a damp track, with Hamilton on pole, Sergio Perez sharing the front row and Max in P3. They were conditions that suited both Verstappen and Hamilton and as the lights went out it was Max not Checo challenging the Mercedes into Turn 1. An overhead shot showed they had both left Perez a long way behind in the braking zone. Going through the corner neither car would yield, wheels came together and Lewis was bumped out over the kerbs with Max taking the lead. The stewards looked at it and decided no action was necessary.

In the early phase of the race Max edged out a five-second lead over the Mercedes, which was struggling to get heat into its tyres. This was evidenced by Valtteri Bottas whose Merc was marooned in mid-pack, unable to make progress. However by the time of the first pit-stops Lewis was moving back into contention.

As Verstappen's inters wore down, so the cooler-running Mercedes' Pirellis had more tyre life left. By Lap 26, Lewis had the gap down to two seconds and was beginning to lap a second quicker than the Red Bull. The drying track was just about ready for slicks.

Red Bull were forced to bring Max in and completed a typically rapid tyre change. They needed Max to keep track position, because going a few centimetres off the dry line could mean a trip to the gravel, as both Perez and

Hamilton later demonstrated. Anyone who wanted to overtake would have to do so with slicks on wet tarmac, so keeping P1 was imperative.

Lewis was on a charge, though. Had the Mercedes team replicated Max's pit-stop time it would have been Hamilton in front, taking control of the dry line. But a front wheel stuck and as Hamilton applied throttle, wagging the rear end at the pitlane exit, he was passed comfortably by the RB17.

The race was red-flagged a lap later when a struggling Bottas edged George Russell's Williams onto the grass and the pair collided. Max controlled the re-start and was even more assured of the win now (even escaping a sideways moment at Rivazza trying to warm his tyres). While Bottas and Russell were exchanging words and suitable gestures, Lewis had been pushing too hard on his new tyres too soon. He slid off into the gravel at the Tosa hairpin, falling back to ninth place.

Hamilton spent the rest of the race recovering his way to P2 while Verstappen's win was a real statement of intent for the season. Red Bull had lost by a narrow margin at the first race in Bahrain, but now they had won a race that should have gone Mercedes' way. Max had shown that he was not going to be intimidated by the world champion. It was 44–43 to Lewis in the drivers' table. Game on.

BELOW: Imola was eerily quiet for the return of Formula 1 after a year's absence.

BELOW LEFT: Lewis and Max: Two masters of wet conditions, but Max kept it on the island.

'It might be a chassis change,' Christian Horner consoled him, 'and Hamilton's down in P7.'

Leclerc never made the start on Sunday. On his way to the grid Ferrari discovered a driveshaft failure, leaving Max effectively in pole position for the race, but from the dirty side. Once he'd cleared Bottas into St Dévote it was his race to control. Finally he had won Formula 1's most prestigious race. His girlfriend, Kelly Piquet, was there to share the joy of winning and a thousand images of the couple embracing and kissing – or trying to within Covid restrictions – were captured.

When he'd got his breath back Max admitted it had been a battle of concentration: 'To keep your focus for so many laps is the hardest part because it's easy to relax when you're in the lead and make a mistake. So you have to keep reminding yourself to keep your thoughts on the road and stay focused.'

In contrast, Azerbaijan was a nightmare. Leading the race from Sergio Perez on Lap 47 of 51, Max experienced a high-speed deflation of his left-rear tyre on the

long Baku straight. It pitched his car into the barriers at 200mph and brought out the red flag. Max was fortunate to walk away nothing more than irritated, giving his deflated Pirelli a parting kick.

To his great relief on the re-start, Lewis Hamilton inadvertently knocked a brake balance switch and steamed into the run-off area, his brakes and tyres smoking. Checo took the win while Mercedes came away with a dismal 12th and 15th.

Things would improve dramatically for Max over three weekends in late June and early July, when the F1 calendar had slotted the French, Styrian and Austrian Grands Prix together for three back-to-back races. The last two were both held at the Red Bull Ring, near Spielberg, and Max was able to capitalize at his most familiar track. He put his RB17 on pole for all three races and won all three races, the last two driving away from the field while the rest of the pack squabbled over the podium places.

After Azerbaijan he had led Hamilton by four points. Heading to Silverstone for the British Grand Prix he had a 32-point lead. It would have been more if Perez had

BELOW: Losing it on the 2.2km-long straight in Azerbaijan is a frightening experience, and Max was lucky the car stayed upright.

BELOW RIGHT: It wasn't funny at the time, but Max shows exactly what he thinks of his Pirelli tyres in Baku.

been able to put himself between Max and his championship rival, but even equipped with Max's data, Sergio was unable to replicate the times Max could put in.

The race at Silverstone brought the rivals into bitter conflict. When Max won the Sprint race on Saturday, Lewis knew that he had to be ahead of his rival before the long Wellington Straight on the opening lap of the grand prix, or he would be gone. He'd also been bullied out of places by Max at Portimao, Barcelona and Imola, so if he was going to make a decisive move it would have to be on the opening lap.

Copse Corner is spectacularly fast. Stand on the outside banking there for a first glimpse of an F1 race and it appears inconceivable that anyone could overtake there. The fact that Hamilton passed Norris and Leclerc at Copse in the same race – in Leclerc's case, giving up the win – is testament that it can be done. But it involves a certain amount of complicity from the car being overtaken, and as Max has shown since his karting and Formula 3 days, he doesn't do complicity.

In this case it sent Verstappen heading for a 51g impact with the barriers, his biggest ever accident.

'Is Max okay?' Lewis asked his engineer Peter 'Bonno' Bonnington hesitantly on team radio. 'He's out the car,' was the reply.

Max wasn't okay. He was physically in good shape for such a heavy impact, but he was furious. And he would get his revenge.

As if to deepen Red Bull's pervading sense of injustice, at the following race, the Hungarian Grand Prix, an inept start from Valtteri Bottas wrecked Red Bull's plan for an immediate strike back. Starting slowly from P2 on a wet grid, the Finn was passed by the Red Bulls and Lando Norris's McLaren before Turn 1. Bottas missed his braking point, shoved his car into the gearbox of Lando's car, which in turn ricocheted into Verstappen's car. Bottas careened on through and clunked into Perez. Sergio out on the spot. Max back in the pits with extensive damage to be repaired under the inevitable Red Flag.

Lewis could only manage a second place in the grand prix, after Formula 1's loneliest re-start. With a drying track everyone took to the pitlane for slicks after the formation lap, leaving the bizarre sight of a singular Mercedes on the grid on intermediate tyres waiting on its own for the lights.

There was rain again in Belgium and no racing at all on the Sunday, with a sodden procession in grid order behind the safety car. When Bernd Mayländer had ticked off enough laps in the red Mercedes AMG GTR to count for half points the race was brought to a conclusion in near darkness. Max had been on pole, so took the win.

ABOVE: Mercedes and Red Bull were neck and neck at Silverstone and Lewis was under pressure to get a result at his home race.

His next win would be far more enjoyable, pushed all the way at his home race, the redesigned Zandvoort, packed to its 105,000 capacity. Max took pole by 0.038 seconds in front of Lewis Hamilton and Valtteri Bottas and so while Mercedes could play the alternative strategy game, Verstappen's team-mate was nowhere to be seen, back in P16.

He didn't need him. With two laps to go Hamilton, who had been close for most of the race, gave up the fight to have a shot at Fastest Lap. Max crossed the line to an explosion of orange smoke canisters as 104,900 Verstappen fans cheered the win. He had completed a clean sweep of all his home grands prix – Monaco, Belgium and the Netherlands – and he had retaken the lead in the drivers' title race by three points.

On to Monza and Max started from the front row alongside former team-mate Daniel Ricciardo's McLaren. Having spent a lot of the season overshadowed by

TEAM-MATE STATS

It's been an uneven contest for the last five years between Max and the second Red Bull seat, although Alex Albon got reasonably close in the latter half of 2019. Hindsight is a wonderful thing, especially in Formula 1, but many in the paddock believe that Alex would have started edging closer to Max had he been given one more season in the senior team. In 2023 Alex outqualified his own team-mate at Williams 22–0.

2019
Max Verstappen vs Alex Albon

	QUALIFYING SCORE	
8		1
	RACES	
5		4
	PODIUMS	
4		0
	POINTS TOTAL	
97		76
	DNFs	
2		0
	BEST QUALIFYING POSITION	
P1		P5
	BEST RACE RESULT	
P1		P4

2020
Max Verstappen vs Alex Albon

	QUALIFYING SCORE	
17		0
	RACES	
12		5
	PODIUMS	
11		2
	POINTS TOTAL	
214		105
	DNFs	
5		1
	BEST QUALIFYING POSITION	
P1		P5
	BEST RACE RESULT	
P1		P3

2021
Max Verstappen vs Sergio Perez

	QUALIFYING SCORE	
20		2
	RACES	
19		3
	PODIUMS	
18		5
	POINTS TOTAL	
395.5		190
	DNFs	
2		2
	BEST QUALIFYING POSITION	
P1		P2
	BEST RACE RESULT	
P1		P1

2022
Max Verstappen vs Sergio Perez

	QUALIFYING SCORE	
18		4
	RACES	
17		5
	PODIUMS	
15		11
	POINTS TOTAL	
454		305
	DNFs	
1		2
	BEST QUALIFYING POSITION	
P1		P1
	BEST RACE RESULT	
P1		P1

2023
Max Verstappen vs Sergio Perez

	QUALIFYING SCORE	
20		2
	RACES	
20		2
	PODIUMS	
21		9
	POINTS TOTAL	
575		285
	DNFs	
0		2
	BEST QUALIFYING POSITION	
P1		P1
	BEST RACE RESULT	
P1		P1

Lando Norris, the Aussie showed an unusual turn of pace off the line, taking the lead and leaving Max to argue with Lewis Hamilton for second place into the Della Roggia chicane. Max gave Lewis a friendly nudge over the kerbing which dropped him behind Lando Norris. Nothing wrong, said the stewards.

For once Red Bull's exemplary pit-stop machine faltered and at Verstappen's first stop the RB 17 was stationary for 11 seconds, changing a stubborn front right. When Lewis Hamilton emerged from his own pit-stop he was ahead, but with Max rapidly closing on the outside as they braked for Turn 1. Lewis turned in in front. Max, on the outside, tried to cut the corner but in doing so mounted the 'sausage kerbing' which launched his car into and on top of the Mercedes. Both cars stumbled into the gravel on exit, with the RB 17 piggybacked on the Silver Arrows car.

Just as Sky Sport's Martin Brundle had viewed Lewis's Silverstone crash as a racing incident, so he absolved Max of blame in the Monza collision.

'Did Max get a bit cheeky in the second part of the chicane?' asked commentator David Croft. 'Max hasn't done anything wrong there,' replied Brundle.

The stewards looked at it in detail after the race and reported their findings very much in the manner of a policeman recording a road traffic accident: 'The driver of Car 44 was driving an avoiding line although his position caused Car 33 to go onto the kerb', they wrote, but they also... 'observed that Car 33 was not at all alongside

Car 44 until significantly into the entry into Turn 1. In the opinion of the Stewards, this manoeuvre was attempted too late for the driver of Car 33 to have "the right to racing room".' Max would take a three-grid place drop for Sochi, which would prove no problem at all.

More importantly, the Halo device had saved Lewis's life. It took an impact from Max's rear tyre and there are uncomfortable photos that show the Pirelli bearing down on Hamilton's helmet. Lewis's fans cried foul and that Max hadn't hung around to see if he was okay. But Car 44 was trying to reverse out of the gravel (very difficult with another car on your rear wing), and that would have been a strong indicator that he was.

In Russia Red Bull decided to double down on the grid penalty by taking an engine change, yet Max stormed through the field from the back of the grid to claim P2. Onwards to Turkey and a rare appearance for the underused Istanbul Park circuit, with its amazing quadruple-apex Turn 7. Hamilton took his own engine penalty and struggled to fifth place. Max followed Bottas home to bank eight more points than Lewis.

With a nailbiting win in Austin and an assured win in Mexico City, Verstappen's lead in the title race was up to 19 points with four races to go. Team Verstappen dared to dream. Nobody could afford a DNF now, least of all Lewis.

But then Hamilton won in Brazil, Qatar and Saudi Arabia. Max was second in all three. It was punch and counterpunch. Indeed in Brazil Max managed to pull an extraordinary block into the fast downhill Descida do Lago (lake descent) turn, running both himself and Hamilton off the track and not incurring a penalty. 'Michael, that's all about "let them race",' Red Bull team manager Jonathan Wheatley quickly appealed over team radio to Race Director Michael Masi. And he got away with it.

In Saudi Arabia there was another incident where Max effectively brake-tested Lewis after Verstappen was

asked to hand the lead back to Hamilton through an illegal move. Max was well aware that a retirement or a broken front wing for the Mercedes would have given him a big points gap for the final race. Lewis was caught off guard. But the clunk Car 33 got from Car 44 was not enough to dislodge Car 44's front wing.

And so it came down to the final race in Abu Dhabi. Both drivers on 369.5 points, it was winner takes all. Late in the race Max found himself in P2 stuck in a safety car queue, with brand new tyres, facing the gearboxes of a lot of lapped cars. It had been the Red Bull team's last roll of the dice to change tyres for a last dash to the flag. It looked to be all in vain. On the road, several cars ahead, leading the race, was Lewis Hamilton's Mercedes. He hadn't dared change his worn Pirellis. When the race got going again – if the race got going again – even banzai Max wouldn't have time to clear the lapped cars to get at Lewis.

But miracles do happen.

The silken-tongued Red Bull team manager Jonathan Wheatley had a way with Michael Masi. Back in the Belgian Grand Prix, run in torrential conditions, Sergio Perez had crashed on the way to the grid. His car had been recovered on a transporter, but Masi wouldn't let him start the race, which had been delayed because of water streaming across the circuit. A patient and explanatory Wheatley pointed out (quite rightly) that he could.

TOP LEFT: Lewis Hamilton may have been a fierce competitor in 2021, but he was also a gracious loser.

ABOVE: Jos with Max after the race, as the reality of what he has achieved finally dawns on him.

RIGHT: Old friends Richard Pex (left) and Thierry Vermeulen (right) are waiting to greet him in Abu Dhabi, but it's Kelly who's centre stage.

At the end of the Abu Dhabi Grand Prix Jonathan got on the radio to Masi to suggest that instead of letting all the lapped cars be allowed past the race leader, as per the rules, why not let the cars between Max and Lewis past...? 'Let them race'. That was the core philosophy of F1. There wasn't time for all the lapped cars to make it through and surely nobody wanted to see such a titanic world championship end behind a safety car...

With the offending lapped cars cleared out of the way, and Mercedes going ballistic, Max calmly picked off Lewis in what was now an uneven contest for the win.

The words came over the radio from Christian Horner with exactly the same euphoria as he'd celebrated Vettel's surprise win of 2010 at Abu Dhabi: 'Max Verstappen, you are the World Champion!'

7

FAMILY MATTERS

PREVIOUS PAGE:
Celebrating world
championship No.3
in Qatar, 2023.

LEFT: Victoria Jane
Verstappen with
father Jos watching
from trackside at Spa
in 2015.

RIGHT: A photo from
April 1997. Sophie
Kumpen sitting with
Noriko Salo, wife of
Mika Salo. Mika
and Jos were
team-mates at Tyrrell
for the 1997 season.

I n the documentary *Whatever it Takes*, there is a
sequence where Max's mother, Sophie Kumpen, lights a
candle in the local church and sends Max a picture of
it. It's a ritual she started before the race in Spain in 2016,
his first grand prix for the senior team. She said she had a
sense he needed some protection. It's something that his
sister also does.

Both mum and daughter try and get to races but for
Victoria it is more complicated now she is the mother of boys
Luka and Lio – with the elder Luka looking uncannily like his
Uncle Max. Growing up and witnessing the attention paid to
her elder brother would be tough for any child and Victoria
was not immune.

'It was hard for me at times. I felt less important. Everything
was about Max,' she revealed in the documentary.

Italy is the centre of the karting world, and before Max was
twelve, the family went to Italy nearly every weekend for
important kart races. Friday afternoon Max would get out of
school around 3pm, Jos would be waiting with the van. They'd

drive straight to Italy, only arriving in the early hours of the morning. Karting practice would be on Saturday, races on Sunday and then there was the long drive back home through Sunday night.

Sophie would follow them home with Victoria – it was her presence on the auto-route behind Jos and Max that legitimized Jos driving off alone from a fuel station to 'teach his son a lesson', even though, as Max points out in a recent father-and-son interview, 'you did come back'.

Sophie's presence was a calming influence, her good nature balanced against Jos's volatility. When they divorced, she could easily have wrecked the whole Verstappen project. It's unusual in any divorce for the family to be split up, one child with each parent, especially where the father sends abusive texts to his wife and is given a restraining order.

'I had to let Max go with Jos,' Sophie admits. 'I knew that if Max wanted a career [in motorsport], he needed to be with Jos. That was a very tough decision emotionally, because I had to let one child go.'

Max, drawing on the emotional intelligence gifted from his mother, is aware that his family have all made sacrifices to get him where he is today.

'It's only natural that I can now give back to my family. It wasn't always easy for my sister and my mother.'

It wasn't easy for his mother to see him turn his back on Belgium, either. He was born in Belgium, lived in Belgium, went to school in Belgium and spent more time on the Genk track in Belgium than anywhere else.

TOP LEFT: Sophie with Victoria and husband Tom Heuts in the Red Bull garage.

ABOVE: Max makes sure he speaks to half-sister Blue Jaye Verstappen after qualifying for the 2023 Belgian GP.

ABOVE RIGHT: Jos, Max and grandfather Frans Verstappen at the tail-end of Max's karting career.

Without Sophie's agreement to let Max go his own way, it's unlikely there would be Max Verstappen, world champion. Some of Jos's behaviour post break-up would have entitled her to slam the door on all but the occasional access to his son. She realized that would not be in her son's interest – and she was right. But it meant that he would become a Dutch sporting icon, not a Belgian one.

Apart from the gift of his mother's racing DNA, his success has come about through the single-minded dedication of his father. Jos was a Dutch motorsport hero (few rookies get two podiums in their debut year, not even Max). Max's reflected fame came from the Netherlands, his racing licence was Dutch and he spent a lot of his formative years hanging out with the Pex family at the workshop they shared in Maasbracht. Max is a Dutch passport holder and cemented that Dutchness in 2022 by becoming an 'officer' in the Order of Oranje-Nassau, an honour awarded for 'longstanding meritorious service to society'.

Without Jos drumming home every single lesson he learned from his own karting and single-seater career it's very unlikely Max would have made it through to Formula 3, let alone become a multiple F1 world champion.

Max is candid about how tough the tough love got. 'My dad was very strict. When I didn't perform, he'd call me names: "idiot, moron, dumb pig. If you're this slow, you're only ever going to be a truck driver." But that did motivate me to get better and prove him wrong. My dad always wanted to get the best out of me. And he certainly did.'

Jos, with his quick-tempered personality and a tendency towards physical altercations when disputes arise, may not have been a great role model for Max, but the roots of that may well have been in his own childhood. Father Frans Verstappen would lock the young Jos in his bedroom. His sister, Gerda Verstappen, related to *de Volksrant* newspaper that, 'Father would have these fits. If he had an argument with Jos they would almost end up fighting.'

Max with his appeasing side, inherited from his mother, was able to absorb the verbal flack during his apprenticeship.

'Even when Max won, Jos wouldn't be happy. He'd get angry and berate him for any mistake he had made or where he could have improved,' remembers Stan Pex. Which is part of the reason he is so unflappable when criticized for some misdemeanour in a race or qualifying. As Max acknowledges, 'the biggest critic I have in my life is my dad, so everything else is just a breeze; it doesn't really matter to me.' Christian Horner would verify this – when he tried to tell Max off about his Baku crash with Daniel Ricciardo, 'it was like water off a duck's back'.

Helmut Marko believes that when Max gets on team radio to have a rant, it is Jos talking. When he apologizes on team radio for that rant, it is Sophie.

Jos's inflexible views on life haven't always been resolved. After a well-publicized bust-up with his father in 2016, when Frans reported his son to the police before withdrawing charges, the duo were never reconciled. Undoubtedly Jos will not have taken kindly to his father's intervention in his grandson's career after he was involved in a nightclub brawl in 2017.

Frans Verstappen told *De Telegraaf* that he sought out a meeting with Red Bull chief Dr Marko. 'I took this step in Max's interest,' Frans told the newspaper, 'because I fear for his career. The only thing I wanted to achieve was that Red Bull intervenes to protect Max from the constant misery caused by his father.' Strong stuff.

Helmut Marko realized the sensitivity of the situation in his response to Frans but didn't wanted to get involved in Verstappen family politics. 'I made it clear that Red Bull has a contract only with Max, and everything else that happens in the family is not our business.'

Suffering cancer, Frans was admitted to a hospice in November 2019 and died the same month. His death came just two days after a triumphant win for Max at the Brazilian Grand Prix.

PIQUETS VS VERSTAPPENS

NELSON PIQUET

European F3:	1st in 1978
Seasons in F1:	14 – 1978–1991
Teams	McLaren(P), Brabham, Williams, Lotus, Benetton
GP Starts:	203
GP Wins:	23
Poles:	24
Podiums:	58
World Championship:	3
24 Hours of Le Mans:	6th GT1 1996

JOS VERSTAPPEN

German F3:	1st in 1993
Seasons in F1:	9 – 1994–2003
Teams	Benetton, Simtek, Tyrrell, Footwork, Honda (Test), Stewart, Arrows, Minardi
GP Starts:	106
GP Wins:	0
Poles:	0
Podiums:	2
World Championship:	0
24 Hours of Le Mans:	1st LMP2 2008

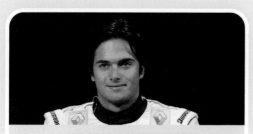

NELSON PIQUET JUNIOR

British F3:	1st in 2004
Seasons in F1:	2 – 2008–2009
Teams	Renault
GP Starts:	28
GP Wins:	0
Poles:	0
Podiums:	1
World Championship:	0
Seasons in Formula E:	5
FE World Championship:	1 – 2014-2015
24 Hours of Le Mans:	4th GT1 2006

MAX VERSTAPPEN

European F3:	3rd in 2014
Seasons in F1:	9 – 2015–2023
Teams	Toro Rosso, Red Bull
GP Starts:	185
GP Wins:	54
Poles:	98
Podiums:	32
World Championship:	3
24 Hours of Le Mans:	Planned entry in GT3 Class

LEFT: Mikaela Ahlin Kottulinsky has gone on to star in the Extreme E series.

BOTTOM LEFT: Max with Mikaela Ahlin Kottulinksy in 2015.

BELOW RIGHT: Dilara Sanlik was waiting in the pitlane to celebrate Max's important Austrian GP victory.

BELOW: Max with Dilara Sanlik watching the Gran Turismo World Tour 2019 Finals in November 2019.

Max is still in regular contact with grandmother, Marianne, and his Aunt Gerda (Jos's sister). In fact he flew them to Japan in 2022 to witness his second world championship triumph. Though he sometimes gets in trouble with his gran for his outbursts on team radio, it's not the string of expletives that upsets her.

At Silverstone one year, he came on the radio to his engineer moaning about the car's performance. Verstappen said: 'I have the pace of an old grandma.' Marianne Verstappen was not having that. 'I had to tell him – I don't drive like an old granny at all.' Even so, it's unlikely she'll be lent his Aston Martin Valkyrie any time soon.

Once freed from the parental shackles of living at home, Max started serious dating. There have been three conspicuous girlfriends in his life. Though notoriously guarded about revealing details of his relationships, Max has been happy to pose with his girlfriends, not just for Twitter/X or Instagram.

The first to be photographed with Max was Swedish touring car driver Mikaela Ahlin Kottulinsky, a seriously fast member of the Red Bull driving programme. When they were dating in 2015 she was competing in the Audi TT Cup, but since has gone on to race for Nico Rosberg's team in the Extreme E series.

After nine months they went their separate ways. Max was then seen out with models Joyce Godefridi and then Roos van der Aa. Perhaps it was the dalliance with lingerie models that persuaded Helmut Marko to introduce Max to the daughter of a

family friend – Dilara Sanlik – though the Austrian denies it. Dilara was less the trophy girlfriend and more the quiet, sincere, take-home-to-mum sort of girlfriend, with impeccable upper crust links – she was a bridesmaid for jewellery heiress Victoria Swarovski (a close friend of Mark Mateschitz).

In January 2018, Sanlik first made an appearance on Max's Instagram page and in September 2018, the two 'officially put a label on it'. They enjoyed winter sports together and Dilara came to races, memorably celebrating Max's win for Honda at the Austrian Grand Prix in 2019.

It was not meant to be.

By late 2020 he was dating Kelly Piquet, daughter of Nelson and eight years his senior. She was also the ex of the man whose career he helped demolish, Daniil Kvyat.

In November of that year, eagle-eyed fans spotted that Max responded to one of Kelly's social media posts.

It has been his longest relationship to date. They have a lot in common, both grew up in and around Formula 1 – they are both 'paddock rats'.

'My girlfriend understands the world I live in, that helps,' Max has said. It has also brought him closer to his mother, as Kelly's mum Sylvia Piquet (a regular face in the pitlane of the 1980s with Nelson) and Sophie Kumpen enjoy nights out with the duo.

Along with Kelly came her daughter, Penelope Kvyat, for whom Max is guardian. Asked by *De Limburger* newspaper if he would one day want kids he was quite open.

'I definitely want children and if they want to race, that's fine. I think I'd approach it differently than how my dad and I handled it though.' Which is hardly surprising. 'The passion he had was quite extreme. He did everything for me: tuning engines, preparing karts. I can't see myself doing that. In any case I'd never push my kids to race. They'll have to want it themselves.'

ABOVE: Kelly Piquet with daughter Penelope at the 2019 Brazilian GP.

ABOVE RIGHT: Almost a full family set: Kelly, Sophie, Victoria, Gran and a lurking Raymond Vermeulen celebrate Max's impressive 2023 Dutch GP win. It helps that photographer Mark Thompson has been photographing Max for years.

RIGHT: In the red flag pause at the 2022 Japanese GP, Max and Kelly pose for the camera.

MAX AND GIANPIERO

One of the highlights of any grand prix weekend is the sometimes testy team radio exchanges between Max and his engineer Gianpiero Lambiase. The duo have worked together since Verstappen replaced Daniil Kvyat in the 2016 season.

With GP's deadpan delivery it's often hard to know where the boundary lies between sardonic engineer and exasperated engineer.

'I think to race engineer Max Verstappen you've got to have strength of character, because he is one tough customer,' Christian Horner said. 'Many race engineers would crumble under that pressure and GP has got the strength of character to deal with that.

'GP is our Jason Statham equivalent, I guess,' said Horner referring to the *Fast & Furious* franchise actor. Though when Max attempts a fastest lap against advice late in the race it does leave Gianpiero quietly furious.

Things came to a head in qualifying for the 2023 Belgian Grand Prix with a rapidly drying track. Spa-Francorchamps is a long lap and there was time left for just three laps. A fast lap, a cooling down lap and a final fast lap. With the track drying and the evolution of lap times rapid, the third lap was going to be the quickest – but Max wanted to put in two laps in a row. His final lap was good enough for P10 and he scraped into Q3, but he was angry.

Verstappen: 'We should have just ****** pushed two laps in a row like I said.'

Lambiase: 'But you are through, Max.'

Verstappen: 'Yeah – I don't give a ****, mate, if I'm through in P10. It was just **** execution.'

Lambiase: 'OK, and then when the track was two seconds quicker for your final lap and you didn't have any energy left, how would that have gone down? But you tell me what you want to do in Q3, and we'll do it. Let me know – sets, fuel, run plan?'

There was a deafening silence. It was blindingly obvious that the Red Bull team call had been correct. After Max had clinched pole by a wide margin in Q3 he got on the radio again.

Verstappen: 'Well, at least we had a good Q3. And sorry GP for being so... on the rant.'

Lambiase: '[I'm] slowly getting used to it, Max.'

In the race they were at it again and GP had to tell his driver to 'use your head more' in the final stint when Max was pushing on too quickly with his new soft tyres. Max joked that he'd like to get far enough ahead so the team could do some pit-stop training. It wasn't well received.

'The problem is that conversation between the two of them, 200 million people are listening to. I mean, sometimes it gets a bit sparky between the two of them. But it'll calm down very quickly,' reassures Horner.

In the past Christian has likened their relationship to an 'old married couple'. 'But there's a great bond and a great trust between the two. There's no counselling required.'

BELOW: Gianpiero studies Max's steering wheel mime carefully.

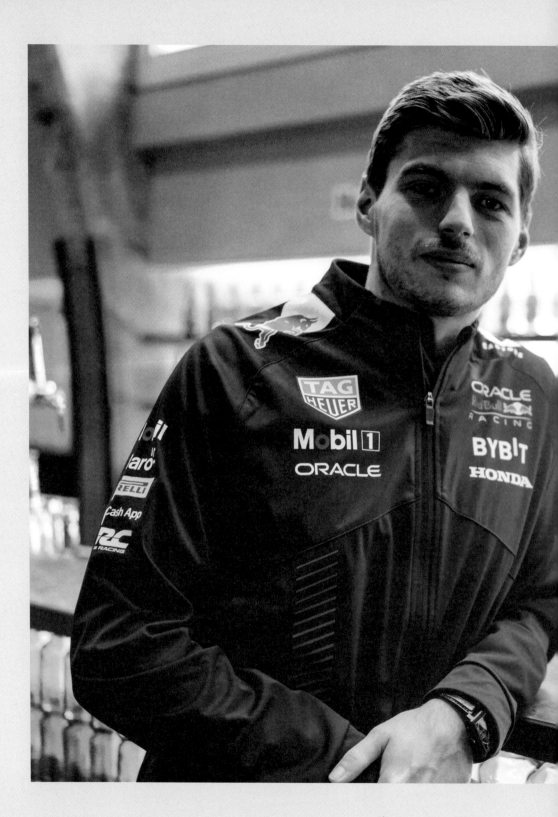

MAKING MONEY

I f the money paid to a Formula 1 driver is an indication of their true talent, then Max Verstappen has long eclipsed seven-time World Champion Lewis Hamilton. With well-funded teams such as Red Bull, Ferrari and Mercedes able to afford the very top drivers, the race to secure the best talent has never been more intense. And Max, of course, is the very best talent.

Since the 2021 season teams have been limited by the financial cost cap. Research has been curtailed, personnel numbers at HQ have been slimmed, and those ever-necessary updates don't flow as regularly through the season. But driver salaries are not included in the budget cap, which means that the area of difference which can bring a significant gain without breaking any financial target is the driver's right foot.

Max plays his earning capacity down and is on record as saying, 'The money doesn't motivate me. All I want is to have a good race on Sunday. If I don't have a good race, the money in my bank account will not make me happy.'

But it will help pay for the private jet home. Only Raymond Vermeulen knows exactly how much Max makes in a year, but with his new Red Bull contract in place until 2028, many think that the grand total is in the region of $55–60m a year. Plus bonuses. And rising.

Even back in 2020, for the *Whatever It Takes* documentary, and without a world championship to his name, Helmut Marko was asked what the difference was between Max in 2015 and Max today. The interviewer clearly expected some kind of performance comparison. The Austrian thought for a second then twinkled, 'The money. Drastically.' Aside from his base salary he will get performance bonuses from Red Bull, plus there are many personal sponsors waiting to get on the train.

PREVIOUS PAGE:
Max at a bar which sells exclusively Heineken Player 0.0. Maybe that's why it's so empty.

LEFT: Formula 1's power couple: Christian Horner and Raymond Vermeulen.

'Dutch people want to join somebody who is winning, and not someone who is having a difficult time,' his old Formula 3 boss, Frits van Amersfoort, told *Autosport*. 'So now that Max is on a high, we tend to forget that we also have a national football team because Max is now the man! That's the truth – they all want to go with a winner.'

In February 2023 Max signed a six-year deal with Heineken to become the face of 'When You Drive, Never Drink' project, promoting alcohol-free lager. The Dutch beer brand has had sponsorship deals in place with Formula 1 since 2016 for their Player 0.0 brand. Indeed, when Max crashed into Lewis Hamilton at Monza it was right in front of a Heineken 0.0 banner.

Heineken CEO Dolf van den Brink saw an immediate synergy between a Dutch lager and a Dutch driver, but explained why they had delayed the approach. 'Max's impact is huge. Formula 1 was originally mainly a European party but is increasingly becoming a global sponsorship platform. Just look at the popularity in America. Internally, there are clear rules about collaborations. We only start working with someone when he or she is 25 years old. Two Dutch icons, that is wonderful.'

Despite having a driver contract to 2028 and a Heineken commercial contract until 2029, Max often likes to flirt with the idea that he might retire from F1 early. When asked to say how long he intends to stick around in the sport, he's quick to cite the travelling he has to do. When Formula 1 published a provisional 24-race calendar for 2024, ending with two triple-headers — three races on successive weekends – he was not impressed.

BELOW: As branding goes, a Dutch icon with a Dutch icon is a pretty perfect fit.

'I've stated before that this is too much and the primary reason I won't keep doing this until I'm 40. All the travelling, it's not healthy,' he told *De Limburger* newspaper. 'I'm still enjoying it now, but there's a lot you have to sacrifice. You're far away from home and the people you love. There comes a point you're done with it.'

George Russell, a friend and occasional padel-playing partner in Monaco (when the gang of Norris, Albon, Russell and Verstappen all have free time), thinks Max's 'whinging' attitude to 24 races is either a negotiating ploy or a signal to the F1 bosses that they can't go on adding races.

'He is the highest paid on this grid and rightly so for what he is achieving but I think it is all a big tactic, his threat of retirement, I hope he doesn't. I hope he stays for as long as I stay because I want to fight against the best drivers in the world.'

Apart from the travel and the sprint format (though you couldn't tell from his sprint results), Max doesn't like the marketing either.

'People may think, "he makes a lot of money, why is he moaning?"' he told *De Telegraaf* newspaper. 'But it's about wellbeing, how you experience things and not how much money you make. I sometimes think I have too many things to do and then I wonder, is it still all worth it? I lose more than a month a year on marketing. At a certain point, you don't want to do it any more.'

In 2022, when he was still 25, he made headlines by becoming the youngest

DRIVER SALARIES

None of the drivers are going to hand over their tax returns, but this is an estimate of what they earned at the start of 2023.

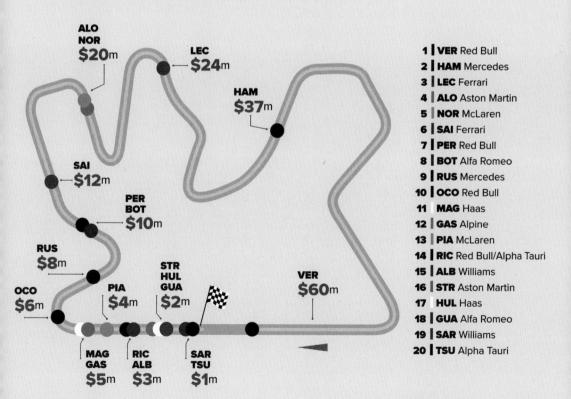

1	**VER** Red Bull
2	**HAM** Mercedes
3	**LEC** Ferrari
4	**ALO** Aston Martin
5	**NOR** McLaren
6	**SAI** Ferrari
7	**PER** Red Bull
8	**BOT** Alfa Romeo
9	**RUS** Mercedes
10	**OCO** Red Bull
11	**MAG** Haas
12	**GAS** Alpine
13	**PIA** McLaren
14	**RIC** Red Bull/Alpha Tauri
15	**ALB** Williams
16	**STR** Aston Martin
17	**HUL** Haas
18	**GUA** Alfa Romeo
19	**SAR** Williams
20	**TSU** Alpha Tauri

ALO NOR **$20**m

LEC **$24**m

HAM **$37**m

SAI **$12**m

PER BOT **$10**m

RUS **$8**m

STR HUL GUA **$2**m

VER **$60**m

OCO **$6**m

PIA **$4**m

MAG GAS **$5**m

RIC ALB **$3**m

SAR TSU **$1**m

person listed on the Quote 500. The Quote 500 is the Dutch version of the Forbes 400, an annual listing of the richest people in the Netherlands, compiled by business magazine *Quote*. Back then he was said to be worth 120 million euros. That figure will not be diminishing despite some eyewatering purchases for the Team Verstappen garage. Along with his Adrian Newey-designed hypercar, the Valkyrie, he has a Ferrari 488 Pista and a Ferrari Monza SP2. You wouldn't get much change out of $6m for those three.

His inclusion on the rich list sparks a familiar round of tax-dodging questions from politicians in the Netherlands. There is an old Dutch saying, 'The tallest trees catch the most wind' and his ever-increasing profile as a three-times world champion and leading Dutch sportsman makes him a big target, even though the majority of F1 drivers have their base in Monaco.

An article in Dutch newspaper *de Volksrant* argued that Max's contribution to the economy of the Netherlands or Belgium is practically zero, considering he has avoided paying taxes in the country for the last seven years. According to the current tax laws in either country, people in the top income tax bracket pay 49.5 per cent tax on income in the Netherlands and 50 per cent in Belgium.

The article estimated that if Max continues to stay in Monaco till 2028, when his contract with Red Bull runs out, his tax avoidance would amount to $200 million over

a period of 13 years. The feature condemned Max for utilizing the benefits provided by the country while growing up, which included his education. Though Jos might argue with that one. 'Every day was a fight to take him to school,' he admitted in 2021. And for the record, St Ursula's is in Belgium.

Max might point out that the far stricter privacy laws in Monaco allow him a degree of anonymity that would be impossible to guarantee at home. Paparazzi are banned in the principality. Even pre-arranged commercial photography takes lengthy organization. His $16m rented apartment in the Fontvieille district of Monte Carlo is also a better location for his girlfriend, who has to balance motherhood with an international modelling career.

Despite the rumblings from left-leaning newspapers, Verstappen's hero status in the Netherlands is undimmed. Take a glance at the list of Dutch sportsmen and women of the year over the last couple of decades and there are a surprisingly high number of speed skaters on the list.

As Dutch cultural commentator Ben Moreno-Broekaert noted, 'I don't think Netflix will be running a series on the high-risk world of international speed skaters any time soon. Max is the undisputed star of one of the highest profile sports on the planet, and he's Dutch. We would have to produce a footballer with the skill of Lionel Messi or a basketball star like LeBron James to equal that kind of status.'

LEFT: The highly desirable Ferrari Monza SP2 can cost between $2m and $3m. That doesn't include servicing.

RIGHT: A flashback to F3 days – Max and Van Amersfoort engineer Rik Vernooij in team apparel with Jumbo branding.

Twan van Gendt is a Dutch BMX champion and a fellow Red Bull athlete: 'In Holland if you go to the local gas station you are definitely going to see something of Max,' he told a Red Bull podcast. 'If you're watching TV and the commercials come on, 70 per cent of the time you see Max – 95 per cent of the population know who Max Verstappen is.'

And walk into the Dutch supermarket Jumbo and you're very likely to meet Max in the beverages section. Though Raymond Vermeulen acknowledges that Dutch companies only like to be associated with success, he managed to persuade Jumbo to take a chance on Max early in his career. They were a sponsor of Verstappen right from his Formula 3 days. The co-sponsor of the Jumbo-Visma cycling team – winner of the Tour de France in 2022 and 2023 – the supermarket's distinctive yellow lettering on a white background has been ever-present on the Verstappen helmet right through to his third world championship in 2023. At which point they stopped.

'Max has now become a global superstar and a true world champion. We're extremely proud to have witnessed this up close, but the international world stage does not suit Jumbo as a Dutch supermarket with stores in the Netherlands and Belgium.' They also quit the cycling team, but it was less about 'mission complete' than the arrest of the CEO in an ongoing money-laundering investigation.

Another lucrative sponsorship comes from Dutch vehicle leasing company, CarNext.com. After his sensational 2021 win in Abu Dhabi, Max and Jos were obliged to drag themselves out of bed the following morning and answer questions from a much perkier David Coulthard. It was all part of the 'Keeping Up With the Verstappens' video series from CarNext.com, looking behind the scenes with Team Verstappen. It didn't take a mind-reader to work out where father and son would rather be as DC rolled out the questions.

Naturally, as a self-confessed sim racing addict, a collaboration with a major games company was an easy sell for Raymond Vermeulen. His initial deal with EA Sports, a division of Electronic Arts, held out the prospect of 'content creation across its product portfolio'.

Americans love winners. 'Max is a tenacious competitor and true champion who shares a deep love of games and play,' trilled Andrea Hopelain, Senior Vice President. 'As he races into Formula 1 history, we are excited to collaborate with him as one of the best athletes in the world to bring more fans together through our EA Sports experiences.'

Max has good language skills and speaks Dutch, English and German and he's also fluent in PR. G-Star RAW clothing, a Dutch brand, has been a Verstappen sponsor since 2019 and Max has his own range of MAXRAW clothes. They're not all orange. Speaking in PR, Max said: 'I've always been a fan of the brand, so it was very easy to get familiar with the G-Star brand DNA. Also, I like the way that we are both always pushing ourselves to improve.'

However, speaking to Channel 4's Steve Jones ahead of the 2023 British Grand Prix Max was a lot more candid: 'Honestly I'm really not interested in fashion. Maybe it comes later, but for me, it's not who I am. I just like to walk around in really chill clothing, an easygoing T-shirt. I don't look in the mirror and think (straightening his lapels) this looks amazing, this looks really cool. I just like to live my life nice and easy.' Maybe he was talking about the extraordinary high-end fashion that Lewis Hamilton is allowed to rock up to grands prix wearing. That's when he's not being a brand ambassador for Tommy Hilfiger.

One aspect of fashion that Max will allow in his life, apart from adding X/Twitter 'likes' to Kelly Piquet's Paris Fashion Week appearances, is his choice of watch. Max is a brand ambassador for team sponsor Tag-Heuer and it's a product he wholeheartedly endorses. Ahead of the 2023 Italian Grand Prix, he dropped in for the opening of their new store in Milan.

Max has his own Verstappen limited edition models of the famous square-faced Tag-Heuer Monaco watch made famous by movie legend Steve McQueen.

'I think it has become almost a tradition now. They started giving me a special one three years ago, the first one in Monaco,' he told Fabrizio Bonvicino from Italian

Watch Spotter.com. 'I think it was the year after I won, something like that. Then they decided to do a new one every year, and that's perfectly fine, because the Monaco is my favourite TAG-Heuer anyway.'

If Max really does hate marketing, then he's prepared to give Tag-Heuer a free pass. 'Every year there are new editions with different details, new materials. So, for me it's like wearing a completely new watch every time,' he enthused. 'Even when you compare my 2–3 Monacos that I have from a few years ago with what I'm wearing now, they are very different – it's still a Monaco, but it's very different.

'They're kind of trophies. I also think it's funny that my father was crazy about watches as he was growing up, really from the time he was a kid ... when I saw my dad's collection I was like "Wow!" this is nice, I want this... and that...

'Then I started earning my own money and over time I was able to put together a nice collection.'

Max has one other rich man's indulgence, his private jet. He reportedly paid $15m for Richard Branson's 15-year-old Dassault Falcon-900EX and decked it out with a distinctive colour scheme of matte dark grey with orange graphics and the Verstappen logo featured on the tail of the plane. Perhaps he was recommended the plane by Didi Mateschitz, who used to pilot one himself.

It's not a status symbol. For Max it's a way of reducing the wearisome time and complication of travelling, plus he can give lifts to friends and relations – also his Monaco-based driver buddies such as Lando Norris, along with Jos and Raymond. Helmut Marko once told the press that Max was so obsessed with his racing

RIGHT: Max, Checo and Christian produce a bee-themed artwork for Sebastian Vettel's 'Buzzin' Corner' at Suzuka's Turn 1 in 2023.

BELOW: As a watch aficionado, Max needed little persuasion to sign up to limited edition Max Verstappen timepieces. He is wearing a version of the classic Tag-Heuer Monaco watch.

BELOW RIGHT: Max's private Falcon jet complete with lion on the tail.

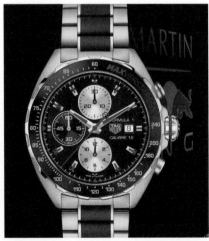

simulator that he had one installed in the jet, a disclosure that Max had to quickly and politely correct. The unspoken aspect of that revelation was that Dr Helmut didn't get lifts home in the Verstappen plane.

The only worrying aspect of Max's luxury transport going forward is that the carbon footprint of a private jet is not good. Lewis Hamilton could afford one, but revealed he had sold it for sustainability reasons. Formula 1 has set itself the target of becoming carbon neutral by the year 2030 and some pressure might be brought to bear.

At Suzuka in 2023 all the drivers were brought together to celebrate Sebastian Vettel's 'bee hotel' initiative, known as 'Buzzin' Corner', and so the eco credentials of the sport are being ramped up in line with a move to cleaner engines from 2026.

Whatever may come to pass, we can be reassured that Max has enough income streams to pay the jet fuel bill going forward.

EVERYBODY LOVES RAYMOND

The second most important member of Team Verstappen is the charismatic Raymond Vermeulen. Raymond is Max's manager, but first and foremost he is a family friend. Raymond was an insurance broker from Roermond who dropped into Grandfather Frans's De Rotonde bar in Montfort in the early 1990s on the search for a kart engine. Max's grandad ran a karting team, which is how Jos got into the sport. Frans did have an engine he could sell the amateur racing enthusiast, but Raymond confessed he wasn't that good with engines and would need someone to install it. Frans said his son Jos could do that.

Thus began a relationship that endures to this day. Jos was managed by former F1 driver Huub Rothengatter, who could be an abrasive character and was often viewed as a stubborn negotiator in dealings with Formula 1 teams. As Jos's career progressed, he involved Raymond more and more in his affairs, to the point where Raymond became Huub's second in command in the management team. People found that they could do business with the far more tractable and diplomatic Raymond.

As a former insurance broker Raymond loves doing deals. In many ways he is like former motorcycle salesman and F1 supremo Bernie Ecclestone, who also never lost his love of 'the deal'. But now Raymond is negotiating with some of the world's leading brands. In the early days of Max's career he was struggling to get sponsorship for his protégé.

At the time of the Florida Winter Series Huub Rothengatter was still a part of Team Verstappen. It was Jos, Huub, Raymond and Max. Given their character profiles it was no surprise that the short-tempered, volatile Jos would sooner or later fall out with the outspoken Huub. At the end of 2014, after Max's successful debut season in Formula 3, the pair ended their business relationship. From that point on, it was Vermeulen who would manage.

When Max arrived to sign his Red Bull contract it was the Verstappen family and Vermeulen present. Despite him being a friend of Jos, Sophie Kumpen regards him as a 'listening ear' for the whole family. 'He is actually the common thread through our life,' she says.

Certainly it is an arrangement unique in F1. There are driver managers (such as Mark Webber managing Oscar Piastri) and international management companies, but Raymond has known Max since he was born.

'Raymond is a trusted person for us all. He's there for Max, he's there for Jos, for me, for Victoria. He's a central point for all of us,' says Sophie.

Jos is always kept in the loop. 'There are certain things I can't say to Max, because of the father-son relationship,' says Jos. 'Raymond does that. I speak to him daily and we discuss everything.'

Vermeulen believes that Max is at the front of the new generation coming to Formula 1. 'He has been, in my opinion, one of the leading figures, through what he's shown on track and engagement with the fans. But it's also the new generation, guys like Charles Leclerc, Carlos Sainz and Lando Norris, attracting a new audience.'

He also believes that three world championships is just the start, telling Formula1.nl in 2023: 'I don't think he's at the top of his game yet. He'll continue to grow. There's more to come.'

MAX'S WINNING TRACKS

Max has been notching up the wins at a range of circuits around the world, especially in the last three seasons. There are 24 circuits on the calendar for 2024 and only a few await a Verstappen victory.

■	5 Wins
■	4 Wins
■	3 Wins
■	2 Wins
■	1 Wins
■	0 Wins

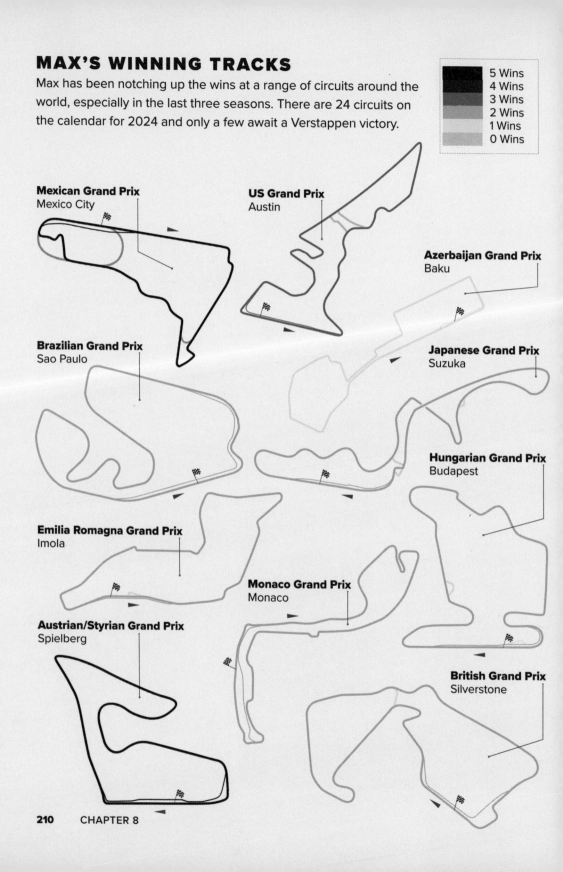

Mexican Grand Prix
Mexico City

US Grand Prix
Austin

Azerbaijan Grand Prix
Baku

Brazilian Grand Prix
Sao Paulo

Japanese Grand Prix
Suzuka

Hungarian Grand Prix
Budapest

Emilia Romagna Grand Prix
Imola

Monaco Grand Prix
Monaco

Austrian/Styrian Grand Prix
Spielberg

British Grand Prix
Silverstone

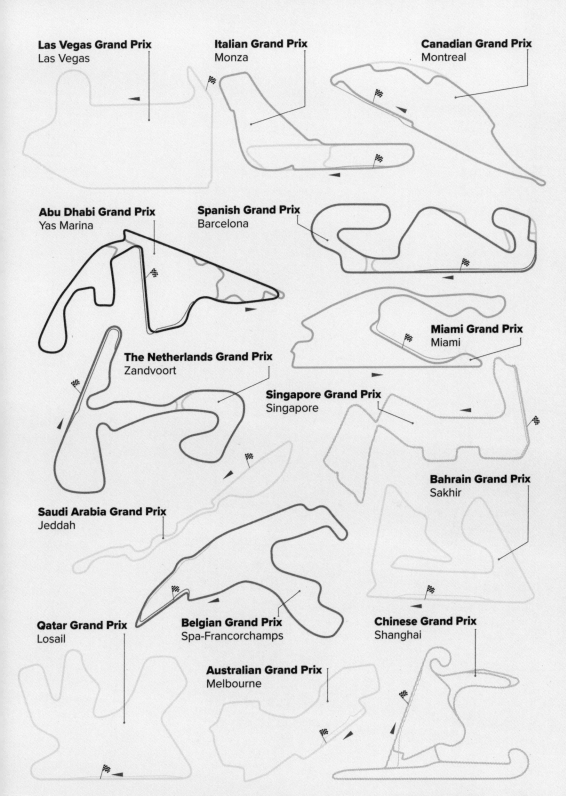

Las Vegas Grand Prix
Las Vegas

Italian Grand Prix
Monza

Canadian Grand Prix
Montreal

Abu Dhabi Grand Prix
Yas Marina

Spanish Grand Prix
Barcelona

Miami Grand Prix
Miami

The Netherlands Grand Prix
Zandvoort

Singapore Grand Prix
Singapore

Bahrain Grand Prix
Sakhir

Saudi Arabia Grand Prix
Jeddah

Qatar Grand Prix
Losail

Belgian Grand Prix
Spa-Francorchamps

Chinese Grand Prix
Shanghai

Australian Grand Prix
Melbourne

THREE IN
A ROW

PREVIOUS PAGE:
A good view of
Max's 2023
celebratory helmet
as he climbs on
board his all-
conquering RB19 for
the main race in
Qatar.

LEFT: A disconsolate
Max walks away
from his stricken car
in Bahrain, for a 19th
place finish in 2022.

I f the 2021 season was tight, the 2022 season was surely
going to be even tighter. This was the year of the new
technical regulations in F1 with a strict set of design
guidelines which allowed cars to follow closer to each other,
hence more overtaking and more of a 'show'. Not that
anyone had been shortchanged in 2021, but it was a move
by Formula 1 to get more cars challenging at the front.

At the centre of the change was a move towards 'ground
effect', with the design of the cars' floors used to create more of
the downforce, effectively sucking the cars to the road. This
was a key element of F1 design from the late 1970s until the
early 1980s. Adrian Newey wrote his university thesis on
aerodynamics and ground effect, so Red Bull were in an ideal
position to exploit that knowhow.

In addition to Red Bull and Mercedes fighting at the front, it
was hoped that Ferrari would step up and maybe Alpine and
McLaren would contest wins on a regular basis.

Right from the reveal at the first Barcelona test, Mercedes
looked to have interpreted the new rules in a different way with
their 'zero sidepod' concept car. Results from the track showed
that it was not the fastest solution and, worse, the car was
bouncing up and down on the straights, 'porpoising'.
Sometimes it was so bad that the drivers' vision became
affected. It impacted other cars, too, but Mercedes were
immediately out of contention for any titles. With the budget
cap in place, they couldn't spend their way out of the problem.

It was Charles Leclerc and Ferrari who became Max's
biggest opposition in 2022. Max's old karting rival took pole
and won the opening round in Bahrain. Max and Checo
suffered fuel system problems, with both cars out before the
end. Next up, Saudi Arabia, and the Red Bull suffered no

technical issues this time. Max was able to duke it out in a gripping battle with Leclerc all the way to the line, winning by 0.5 of a second. In Australia, though, another fuel problem ended his race early as Leclerc took the win. Three races down and Max was already 46 points behind the championship leader. He wasn't even in the top five; both Mercedes drivers were above him.

And this year Checo was a lot closer to his team-mate than 2021. Helmut Marko thought he knew the answer. 'The simplest explanation for this is the new cars with less downforce suit some drivers better and others less. Max finds it even harder. He hasn't found the right balance yet and, therefore, doesn't have the fullest confidence in the car. His aggressive driving style doesn't quite go together with the new cars.'

But then Max won the Emilia Romagna Grand Prix at Imola, and again in Miami, and at Barcelona. And after six races he'd turned the big deficit into a six-point lead over Leclerc.

Monaco was contentious. With qualifying position fundamental to the race result, Perez was ahead of Verstappen in Q3 when he put his Red Bull into the barriers at Portier. That handed Ferrari a front row lock-out with Leclerc on pole and Verstappen only fourth, behind Perez.

In the race, run in wet-dry conditions, Ferrari contrived to mess up their pit-stops from wets to inters to slicks, 'Box, box – no, stay out, stay out!' 'What!' Leclerc slipped from first to fourth, Perez jumped Sainz for the win, and Max came home third. The word 'fiasco' is Italian in origin and it would not be the last time a strategy call would impact on the Scuderia's results.

Max then won in Baku and Montreal – and although Charles Leclerc pegged the lead back with a win in front of the massed ranks of Verstappen fans in Austria, that was the high-water mark of his challenge. If Verstappen had not liked the new car at the start of the season, he certainly loved it now. He took wins in France, Hungary, Belgium, the Netherlands and Italy – giving him a 116-point lead over Leclerc. It was now down to 'when' not 'if' he would clinch his second world championship crown.

ABOVE: Track position is everything at Monaco. Charles Leclerc leads Carlos Sainz, but in 2022 Ferrari contrived to hand the race to Sergio Perez. Max would benefit from serial Ferrari strategy failures.

TOP RIGHT: Leclerc and Verstappen go wheel to wheel in Austria. Charles won the race, but his 38-point deficit was the closest he'd be to Max for the remainder of the season.

RIGHT: Trackside manager Olaf Janssen shares the Abu Dhabi podium with a reflective Charles Leclerc and third-placed Sergio Perez.

THE RACE

FORMULA 1
Japanese Grand Prix
Suzuka International Race Course, Japan
9 October, 2022

It was the Formula 1 race that had everything – but in a bad way. Endless rain, safety cars, a red flag, two extraordinarily dangerous moments, rules confusion and through all the chaos Max Verstappen scored a convincing win. To everybody's surprise he became world champion for the second time before the evening was out.

The conditions at the start of the 2022 Japanese Grand prix were monsoon-like, very similar to the 2014 Japanese Grand Prix in which Jules Bianchi suffered his ultimately fatal accident. The rain that had been predicted to arrive, arrived. Race directors had been powerless to move the start time forward. Global TV schedules first, fans second, racing drivers' safety a poor third. Charles Leclerc was the only driver who stood in the way of Max clinching a second world championship and his

RIGHT: He was worried that his second title was slipping away, and now he'd won it with four races to spare.

BELOW: Max makes a decisive move on Charles Leclerc around the outside of Turn 1 at Suzuka.

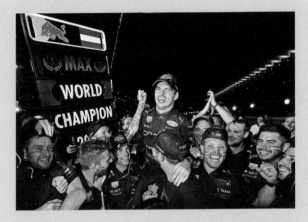

interest in the title was purely mathematical. It was more a question of where Max was going to secure it, not whose name was going to be on the trophy.

Leclerc showed he wasn't giving up on the maths by putting his Ferrari on the front row and when the lights went out got a better launch than Max. He looked to be steaming into the lead at Turn 1, but braked gingerly and Max swept around the outside, unchallenged.

Behind, there was carnage as Carlos Sainz, starting from P3, put his car into the barriers between the hairpin and the fast Spoon Corner. The Ferrari ended up side-on to the track as almost the entire field sped through at 150mph, narrowly avoiding the kind of accident that had claimed Anthoine Hubert's life at Spa in 2019. Some drivers didn't even see him as they passed the stricken car, so bad was the spray.

Pierre Gasly collected part of an advertising hoarding and had to return to the pits for a new front wing. With the safety car dispatched, Gasly raced out of the pits to catch up to the back of the pack only to find a breakdown truck on circuit removing Sainz's Ferrari. The Frenchman, who was a close friend of Hubert, was incandescently angry. This shouldn't have happened. Least of all at Suzuka. Red Flag.

After a pause the race re-started behind the safety car and once the light had switched to green and drivers had swapped their compulsory wets for inters, Max drove away from his pursuers at a second a lap. All attention was now on the battle between Sergio Perez and Charles Leclerc for second place, right up to the time-imposed limit of Lap 28. When Charles cut the final chicane to keep ahead of Checo, he got a five-second penalty that demoted him to P3.

As the race had run to just 28 of its scheduled 53 laps, everyone was expecting half points. So Max would have to wait. But then it was revealed that as a re-started race it could be awarded full points. Leclerc had lost his mathematical fight. In the damp, darkening gloom of post-race Suzuka, Max could celebrate his second world crown. It had been a calm, error-free win in tricky conditions. And it was made more timely as Dietrich Mateschitz got to witness his sixth Red Bull drivers' championship title. Thirteen days later, the reclusive billionaire with a passion for F1 racing passed away from pancreatic cancer aged 78.

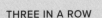

Family Verstappen were all flown out to Japan (see Greatest Races page 218) and with the RB 18 excelling in the high-speed corners of Suzuka Max duly delivered the win that confirmed what everyone not in Red Bull team colours had been talking about since Round 9.

A curious footnote to the final race in Abu Dhabi was that Charles Leclerc was able to stay ahead of Sergio Perez in the battle for second in the drivers' table. In Brazil, the penultimate race, Max had refused to give up sixth place after Perez had let him through to attack Alonso in front. When GP asked him to swap back, Max was blunt. 'I told you already last time, you guys, don't ask that again to me. Okay? Are we clear about that? I gave my reasons and I stand by it.'

It didn't make for good audio and hinted at some festering dispute. It was only for sixth and seventh places. Max was already on course for breaking the all-time record for points scored – the press sensed a story. Why had something so routine provoked such a strong reaction? There was speculation that the dispute had arisen from Monaco and that Checo's spin in qualifying had not been altogether accidental. Christian Horner did his best to dampen down the story, while quietly longing for the days he had Daniel Ricciardo in the second car.

ABOVE: Christian Horner, 'the Usain Bolt of Red Bull team photos', exits the end of term celebration at speed in Yas Marina.

RIGHT: Max leads away at the start of the 2023 Dutch Grand Prix as the rain starts to fall.

2023 Breaking More Records

The theory of F1 technical evolution is that the longer the rules stay the same, the closer the racing should get. Thus after the big rule changes of 2022, the rest of the teams would copy the best bits of the world championship-winning car, the Red Bull RB18, and 2023 would not be the cakewalk that Max Verstappen enjoyed in 2022...

Essentially the theory proved correct. Mercedes finally abandoned their zero sidepod concept after making little progress in the early races of 2023 and spent the rest of the year clawing their way back to the front. But the rest of the grid had closed up. At Round 5 in Miami, Sergio Perez was fastest in Q1 with a 1:27.713 lap. Slowest was Logan Sargeant in the Williams with a 1:28.577 – that meant there was just 0.864 of a second between P1 and P20. Formula 1 had never ever seen

THE RACE

FORMULA 1
Dutch Grand Prix
Circuit Zandvoort, Netherlands
27 August, 2023

Max Verstappen's seemingly effortless stroll through the 2023 season brought a number of F1 records into sharp focus. By Round 13, he'd been on the top step of the podium since the Miami Grand Prix in May and winning at his home race on 27 August would equal Sebastian Vettel's record of nine wins in a row, a remarkable achievement.

Surely it would be a formality? The fact that he might do it in front of a home crowd, 97 per cent of them Verstappen fans, including the Dutch royal family, added to the excitement, but also the pressure.

The rest of the grid were still to come to terms with Adrian Newey's RB19, but in any race the fastest car can be tripped up by a number of things; McLaren's perfect season of 1988 had been ruined by a backmarker ignoring blue flags. It could be a botched pit-stop, an ill-timed safety car, a technical problem or, most hazardous of all, a wet-dry race. The Dutch Grand Prix was a wet-dry-wet race which added an extra layer of jeopardy. The crowd may have come expecting to celebrate a win, but it would not be easy.

Verstappen started from pole and as the lights went out and with the whole of the grid on rapidly cooling slicks the rain started to fall and intensify.

'It is hammering it down on the main straight! This is nearly impossible!' exclaimed C4 commentator Alex Jacques. 'They will have to go to the pits or they will lose so much time,' chimed in David Coulthard.

Sergio Perez did. Max didn't. Some of the cars stayed out thinking it would be a brief shower, but the track was now too wet for slicks. When Max

BELOW RIGHT: Torrential rain brought a stop before full distance.

BELOW: Max and Willem-Alexander. On the podium, the national anthem was sung by Emma Heesters, and something fans don't often see, Max was visibly moved. Dutch F1 presenter Olav Mol commented: 'Something we've never seen before. Quivering nostrils, tears in his eyes.'

came out after the second lap on inters, the timing screens showed him back in P11 just as Perez took the lead from the slick-shod George Russell.

Max had to negotiate his way past cars who were bravely hanging on on slicks, plus pass the early stoppers who'd jumped him with their early stop for intermediates. Given his love of the wet, his knowledge of the track and spurred on by the Oranje Army he carved into Perez's lead. By Lap 10, he was less than five seconds behind Sergio and with a drying track Red Bull brought him in early for a change back to slicks. The undercut was so great that even when Checo was brought in a lap later, he rejoined to find Max three seconds in front.

All was looking 'simply lovely' until eight laps before the end of the race when another intense shower deluged rain across the track. Cars, including Perez's Red Bull, went aquaplaning off the road at the end of the main straight. Red Flag.

At the re-start, Max had to hold off a resurgent Fernando Alonso to cross the line in front of his damp-yet-jubilant fanbase. It had been a commanding win in the trickiest of conditions. By contrast, the record-breaking 10th win at the next race in Monza was a walk in the royal park.

Very few sports stars get to be hugged by Dutch King Willem-Alexander, but it was a day of high national emotion.

MOST WINS IN A SEASON

In a season where Max broke the record for successive wins, he also anihilated the record for the most wins in total, beating his own previous mark of 15.

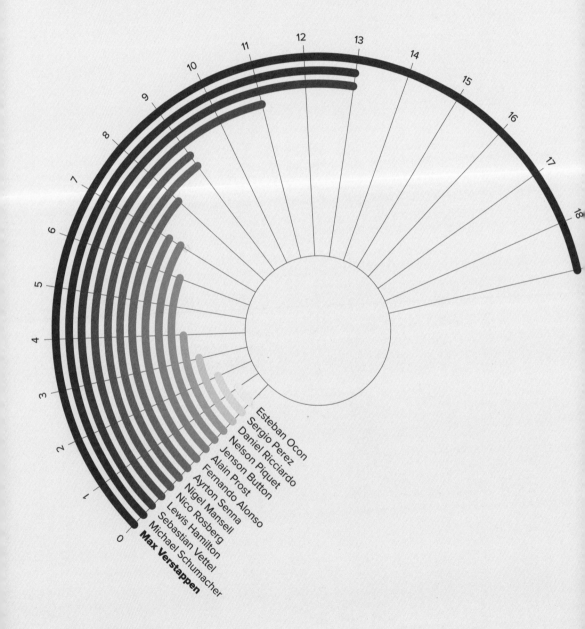

that kind of tight qualifying margin, when a missed apex could send a driver plunging ten places down the grid.

The rest of the field may have been close, but it was still Max in the Red Bull RB 19 showing the way in Bahrain, the opening round. Red Bull locked out the front row and came home a dominant 1–2, Max from Checo. Their closest competitor was Fernando Alonso's Aston Martin thirty seconds back. In Saudi Arabia Perez reversed the order in another Red Bull 1–2. Max won his first Australian Grand Prix in Round 3, but Sergio bounced back in Baku to win the Azerbaijan Grand Prix.

It was while following Perez in Baku that Max resigned himself to bring the car home second (very un-Verstappen-like) and started playing around with settings on his steering wheel. Treating the latter half of the race as a practice session, he actually found a set-up solution to suit his driving style. Jos discussed the adjustments with his son after the race in Baku: 'He said, "I think I've found it now, what we need to do".'

The next race was Miami – another street circuit likely to suit Perez. Checo put his RB 19 on provisional pole and Max, who had been quicker than his team-mate in Q1 and Q2, was gearing up for a final banzai run in Q3 when Charles Leclerc crashed and the session was red-flagged. It left him down in ninth place on the starting grid. When the lights went out, Verstappen thundered through the field before grabbing the lead on Lap 21.

It was a terrible psychological blow for Perez, who had entertained hopes of running Max close for the title. If he couldn't beat him on a street circuit – his speciality – then it would be tough to challenge at races where Verstappen traditionally shone. Miami was the start of Verstappen's incredible run of ten successive grand prix wins, all aided by the lessons learned in Baku.

Helmut was typically brutal about Perez's subsequent dismal performances. 'He has now woken up from his world championship dream. Maybe that will help him to focus again on delivering the best possible performance.'

Verstappen's record-breaking run climaxed in Monza at the Italian Grand Prix, a far more straightforward race victory than the previous round at Zandvoort where a

sudden rain shower caused havoc at the start (see Greatest Races page 222). Any notion that Max would have a serious challenger in 2023 had been dismissed the moment Perez fell off the pace.

He was annoyed by his rivals claiming that the RB19 had been designed purely to suit his driving style and that making the car Max-centric had disadvantaged Sergio Perez.

'I just drive the car I get the fastest way possible. I'm not there to tell the guys to give me more front end, because that's how I like it,' he told reporters at Monza. 'I'll just say "design me the fastest car, and I'll drive around that." Every single year it's just different, every car drives a little bit different. People will say "what is your driving

ABOVE: Max's pitcrew celebrating in Qatar after his sprint race points clinched the title with five races to go.

ABOVE RIGHT: The core of Team Verstappen in Qatar: Raymond, Max and Jos with celebratory T-shirts.

style?" My driving style is not something particular, I adapt to what I need for the car to go quick.'

Christian Horner, naturally, agreed. 'I think that the good drivers adapt. You see it in wet conditions, mixed conditions, varied conditions. The elite, they adapt quickly. I think that's one of (Max's) key skill sets. His ability to adapt to the feeling and the grip levels that a car gives him.'

At 2023 season end Adrian Newey give a wide-ranging interview to the BBC's Andrew Benson, reflecting on the success of the Red Bull RB19, and, as usual, deflecting the praise towards other people.

'I have been fortunate enough to have worked with several great drivers,' he said, 'and while their personalities can be significantly different in how they conduct themselves – their approach to little things like debriefs after each session – the thing they all have in common is the ability to drive the car with a lot of mental reserve left.

'They are able to drive the car with enough capacity left over to think about how they are using the tyres, how the race is unfolding, when to push, when not to push, more of course now in particular with these cars, how to adjust the electronics settings to suit the handling of the car as it develops through the race. Max is quite exceptional at that.'

And the bad news for his rivals is that this racing intelligence is just going to keep getting more refined in seasons to come.

**WHAT
LIES
AHEAD**

I n 2021 he edged it. In 2022 he was challenged and took control. In 2023 he smashed it out of the park. There is little doubt that in the next two years Max will continue to break records with the Red Bull RB20 and RB21.

The chilling fact for Verstappen's rivals is that he has added to his arsenal of talents – namely his natural speed and his ability to judge a race track from the earliest of laps. He has now learned to be patient and bide his time. It hasn't stopped him swearing, but as Helmut Marko says, 'When he gets in the car he's a completely different person.' The ever-developing Max is more calculating, able to balance risk and reward.

He still has grands prix where qualifying sessions don't go quite as planned, or when engine units need replacing and he is cast down the grid. In those instances, such as the 2023 Belgian Grand Prix, his peerless overtaking skills were immediately to the fore. He makes it all look effortless, while team-mates with the same machinery struggle.

Another advantage that Max enjoys is his long-running relationship with race engineer Gianpiero Lambiase – the duo have been together since 2016. 'After I say I have a bit of understeer or oversteer, GP knows what he will change on the car for me, the way I drive the car as well, and that takes time (to develop),' Max told a Red Bull podcast. 'That's why I would always be against changing race engineers they're crucial in your performance. The longer you can stay together, the better.'

Gianpiero believes their sometimes terse conversations help save time. 'If we have to be blunt about something with each other, we will be, and I think that just fast-tracks you to short-term gains, which ultimately is maximizing the potential of the car during a race weekend.'

The all-out determination to win has been tempered too. In the 2023 Baku race he was outpaced by Sergio Perez, whose ability on street circuits has never been doubted, and an ill-timed safety car left him running second. It was early in the year when the drivers were still learning about the RB19's set-up quirks.

'I knew that it was going to be very hard to pass,' Max admitted after the race. 'So I was trying a lot of things, a lot of different combinations on the (steering) wheel. Some worked, that's why it was a bit of an up and down stint.

'Towards the end of the race, I found my rhythm, I found my preferred balance and it helped to just find a little bit more of an edge. I jumped out of the car after the race, and of course P2 is not where I want to be, but I was like, "I actually learned a lot throughout the race".'

A little (extra) knowledge is a dangerous thing with Max.

As far as team-mates go, whereas in 2023 Max could have won the constructors' championship on his own, Red Bull cannot rely on the other F1 teams messing up so badly. In future he may need a team-mate to back him up. Helmut likes the idea of Max and Lando Norris and has admitted, 'In terms of youth and speed, he would suit us very well.'

Christian Horner looks back fondly at the time Max was paired with Daniel Ricciardo and the team-mates genuinely had a whale of a time – a spark missing from the Perez/Verstappen relationship – but the Red Bull team principal is always

BELOW LEFT: Team Redline's LMP2 entry for the 24 Hours of Le Mans sim race held in June 2020. Max was driving with Lando Norris and Dutch sim racing star Atze Kerkhof.

quick to insist, 'I don't want to talk about other teams' contracted drivers.'

He has Helmut to do that. Marko revealed that he almost signed Norris up before he went to McLaren. 'At Toro Rosso, we had already reached an agreement with him at the time, until his manager realized there was an option for a McLaren contract.'

Lando already goes to races in Max's private jet. In a 2022 Red Bull podcast Verstappen revealed that Norris treats the plane like a glorified golf buggy. 'Lando keeps pestering me to go and play golf with him. He is fully addicted. Yesterday he flew with me here (Baku) and he had his golf clubs with him, because afterwards he wants to play in Montreal.'

They also go sim racing together and along with former Dutch speed skater-turned-sim-racer Atze Kerkhof took part in a simulated Le Mans. And if that wasn't enough, they have one extra thing in common: Cisca Wauman, Lando's mum, is Belgian. It's a natural fit.

BELOW: Lando Norris and Max are the best of friends. But then again, so were Nico Rosberg and Lewis Hamilton before they became team-mates at Mercedes.

Team Verstappen Racing

Formula 1 is not the only motorsport enterprise that Max is involved in. The trio of Max, Jos and Raymond Vermeulen that constitute Team Verstappen – or more correctly Verstappen.com Racing – are pursuing other avenues alongside the main event of Formula 1, and all with Red Bull sponsorship.

Jos is taking part in Belgian national rallying events, while finding time to coach Thierry Vermeulen, Raymond's son, in the DTM (German touring car) championship.

Max has long been the owner of a couple of GT3 cars and wants to put a team together for 2025. Stan Pex, the kart driver who first drove Max to tears at four years old because he was in a kart first, is a likely candidate to join.

'I know who my real friends are. They were also there when you have your tough times and you needed them – and they are still around,' he revealed to Channel 4's Steve Jones at Silverstone. 'For example, after this race weekend my friend – he's still racing in karting – he's flying in Sunday night. And on Tuesday we go private testing with my GT3 cars.'

Max's dismay at a 24-race F1 calendar, apart from the jet fuel it involves, could well be down to the limits it puts on his side projects. In August 2023 he discussed his

LEFT: Jos rallying his Skoda Fabia in Belgium in 2023. The dangers of rallying far exceed those of F1.

BELOW LEFT: Thierry Vermeulen racing in the DTM championship.

BELOW: Max lines up on the Monaco grid in 2015 with a Renault RS01 car, eligible for the GT3 series. Max owns one and treated Jos to a hilarious nerve-jangling ride at Spa.

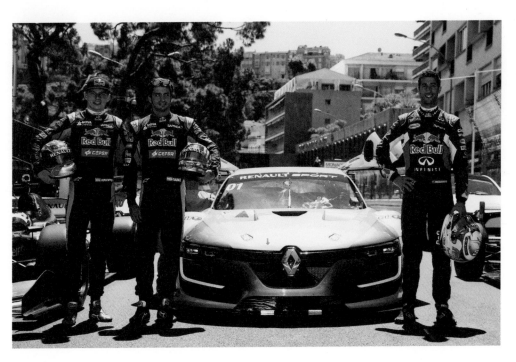

plan for a GT3 team with Dutch magazine *Formule 1*.

'We are working on it at the moment. Next year will be tight, but I would like to have it as soon as possible. Having a GT3 team in 2025 with a minimum of two cars should be possible.'

Max is hoping to scope out potential GT drivers from his sim racing connections. In 2022 he agreed to be part of the very wordy 'Verstappen.com Racing X Red Bull' initiative, which gets more people into sim racing.

'It's about creating a stepping stone from sim racing to GT3, so that you don't have to only go through karting to get into motorsports, because that costs a lot of money at the moment,' he told the magazine. 'We have been working on it for a while. The planning phase is over, we are in action mode now.'

But karting has seen an upsurge too. Maarten van Wesenbeeck is the general manager of the Dutch karting federation and says that Max's success has increased the profile of junior racing. 'Attendance at the karting tracks is higher than a few years ago and we are seeing a marked increase in licence applications. Verstappen has a huge impact on the sport, both through his performance on track and by being someone a lot of children identify with and look up to.'

Unfulfilled Ambition

Many motorsport doors have been opened by Max's unparalleled talent, but his reputation for going flat out from Lap 1 can occasionally backfire. In 2023 Red Bull announced that four-time world champion Sebastian Vettel had signed up for a demonstration run on the fearsome Nürburgring Nordschleife in his 2011 RB7 car. It was all part of a Red Bull motorsport celebration. Alpha Tauri driver Yuki Tsunoda got to drive a Honda NSX GT3 car and dad Jos Verstappen 'delivered a breathtaking performance' in his Ford Supervan 4.2 in front of 35,000 fans on the short circuit.

'I wanted to do it, but I was not allowed by Helmut,' smiled an envious Max. 'He knew that I would try and go to the limits. I would have loved to do it. I heard this event was coming up, and Helmut was sitting at the table and he said: "No, no, no, you're not doing that!"'

Understandably Helmut Marko is keen to protect his major investment. Max and Team Verstappen are deeply embedded in the Red Bull organization and, with a contract until 2028, will be so for many seasons ahead. The Austrian views Max as a talisman.

'A lot of young people want to come to work with the team and that's because of Max. And Adrian Newey. Newey is the holy genius but Max is the emotion.'

Max likes the idea of a settled environment. 'I feel happy here. I really believe in everyone within the team. And yeah, I don't like when you're in the final year of your contract, and you're really leaving it late because then you start creating a bit of an awkward feeling within the team. When you feel happy, there's no reason to leave. Of course, it's a long extension, but I don't see any reason to go somewhere else.'

The long-running joke between Premier League football rivals Arsenal and Tottenham is that Tottenham have the space to host American football games because they don't need a trophy room. At the rate Max is collecting them, the 2028 Red Bull trophy room may well be looking for new premises in Milton Keynes.

THE RACE

FORMULA 1
Abu Dhabi Grand Prix
Yas Marina, Abu Dhabi, United Arab Emirates
26 November, 2023

From Monza onwards, the Singapore Grand Prix was the only exception to Max's total dominance in 2023. He trailed home in a hard-to-comprehend fifth place at Marina Bay. From then on it was back-to-back wins in Suzuka, Qatar, Austin, Mexico, Sao Paulo and Las Vegas. He had been immensely critical of all the razzmatazz surrounding the debut race down the Sunset Strip in Vegas – probably from the moment he was told he would race in Elvis-tribute overalls, but the grand prix had proven to be a thriller, one of the best of the season, and one of his best, too.

As the weary F1 teams assembled in Abu Dhabi a week later, having completed six punishing grands prix in the last eight weeks of the season, Max stood on the brink of motor-racing immortality. F1 records were falling like dominoes.

Yet from the start of the practice sessions, where George Russell dominated, Max and the all-conquering RB19 had struggled to find a balance. Max complained that his car was 'jumping around like a kangaroo'. In fact such was the malaise within the team that Helmut Marko had bet Christian Horner 500 euros that Max wouldn't be able to put his car on the front row in qualifying. Verstappen was only told of the wager once he'd clinched his 12th pole of the year. 'Helmut lost a bet? What world are we living in?' replied Verstappen after being told he was P1.

Helmut would have expected Max's race pace to take him through to the win but as the lights went out Charles Leclerc was able to get alongside and challenge him through the first part of the opening lap. Ferrari were embroiled in a battle for second place in the constructors' title, trailing Mercedes by just four points, so this was not an afternoon for Charles to contemplate wheel banging when second place could be enough.

Leclerc let Max go and from that point on it was a question of managing the tyres on what proved to be a two-stop race. Only the radio report that the engine was pushing back on down changes gave any glimmer of hope that Leclerc might end the season in a blaze of glory. Further down the field there were strategy battles and wheel-to-wheel action rarely seen in the original version of the Yas Marina circuit, but the 25 points were only heading one way after Lap 1.

As Max crossed the line and the fireworks exploded across the Emirates' sky, the final staggering figures could be etched onto stone for a season that is unlikely to be repeated and records that may never be surpassed.

Equipped with Adrian Newey's RB19 Max had beaten his own record of 15 wins in a season, setting a benchmark of 19 wins out of 22 races. He had been on the podium 21 times out of 22 races. He had scored an astonishing 575 points (121 more than last year and a winning margin of 290 points over second place). He had set a new record at Monza for most successive wins with 10 victories. He had beaten Alberto Ascari's win-to-starts ratio that stretched back to 1952. He had become the first driver to lead over 1,000 laps in a season. And incredibly, he was now third on the all-time race winners' list with 54 – having passed Ayrton Senna, Alain Prost and Sebastian Vettel over the course of 2023.

On the slowdown lap Gianpiero Lambiase came on team radio sounding unusually emotional: 'All missions complete. What a year. Well done my friend.'

Max sounded a little choked up, too. 'Another unbelievable race guys ... we did it GP.'

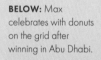

BELOW: Max celebrates with donuts on the grid after winning in Abu Dhabi.

PICTURE CREDITS

ALSO AVAILABLE FOR F1 FANS...

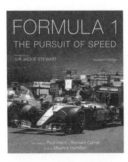

ISBN 9781781317082

ISBN 9781781319468

ISBN 9780711274204

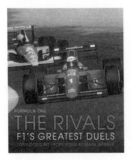

ISBN 9780711280717

ISBN 9780711289499

ISBN 9780711286474